PROJECT-BASED LEARNING

IMPACT™
CALIFORNIA
SOCIAL STUDIES

UNITED STATES
HISTORY & GEOGRAPHY

CONTINUITY & CHANGE

 AVAILABLE ONLINE!

Mc
Graw
Hill
Education

mheducation.com/prek-12

Send all inquiries to:
McGraw-Hill Education
8787 Orion Place
Columbus, OH 43240

ISBN: 978-0-07-682723-7
MHID: 0-07-682723-2

Printed in the United States of America.

1 2 3 4 5 6 QVS 21 20 19 18 17

Table of Contents

ENGLISH PROJECT-BASED LEARNING

CHAPTER 1

Creating a Nation, From Beginnings to 1877

Essential Questions: What characteristics define a society? Why do people form governments? How should societies settle disputes?

CHAPTER 2

War and the West 1844–1890

Essential Question: Why would people take on the challenge of life in the West?

CHAPTER 3

Creating a Modern America 1865–1901

Essential Questions: How did the United States become an industrialized society after the Civil War? Why do people migrate? How is urban life different from rural life?

CHAPTER 4

Becoming a World Power 1872–1917

Essential Question: How are empires built?

CHAPTER 5

The Progressive Movement 1890–1920

Essential Question: Can politics fix social problems?

CHAPTER 6

World War I and Its Aftermath 1914–1920

Essential Question: Why do nations go to war?

IMPACT™
CALIFORNIA SOCIAL STUDIES

Creating Relevancy
with Active Learning

By asking questions, defining interests, and facilitating active participation, students will work at a higher level of involvement and critical thinking than ever before. While participating in hands-on projects, student learning becomes more relevant, exciting, and thoughtful.

Projects in *IMPACT™: California Social Studies*

We believe that the social studies are about doing —
get students thinking, researching, talking, inquiring, and connecting.

IMPACT™: California Social Studies provides a variety of hands-on and digitally focused projects to help you motivate and engage students.

- Deepen students' critical thinking and problem solving skills

- Encourage discourse, teamwork, and collaboration

- Demonstrate relevancy to today and to students' world

DISCOVER IT ALL ONLINE: MHECALIFORNIA.COM

INSTRUCTIONAL PATHWAYS

With the seamless integration of print and online resources, **IMPACT:** California Social Studies provides multiple pathways to engage with the content the way teachers want to teach and the way students want to learn. Whether student-centered or teacher-led, teachers have the flexibility to choose any pathway for any unit of study. **IMPACT:** California Social Studies will help students experience the world and shape the future.

Student Edition   Inquiry Journal   Teacher Edition   Assessment   Digital

Teacher-Directed Path
TEACHER-LED

ESSENTIAL QUESTION

The teacher-directed pathway supports teachers by providing interactive, differentiated activities and providing a linear path through the content. Assessments wrap-up the lessons and chapters in this traditional path.

STUDENT
Reads and considers Essential Question

TEACHER
Introduces Essential Question

Inquiry Path
STUDENT-CENTERED

ESSENTIAL QUESTION

ANALYZE SOURCES & GATHER EVIDENCE

The inquiry pathway encourages students to engage with the essential question by analyzing primary sources, reporting findings, and taking action.

STUDENT
Writes Supporting Questions

TEACHER
Engages with students on the broader themes and issues

STUDENT
Asks additonal questions, analyzes resources

TEACHER
Directs students through extracting evidence, and models source analysis

As students draw conclusions, they may need to circle back and gather more evidence

Project Path
STUDENT-CENTERED

ESSENTIAL QUESTION

INVESTIGATE BACKGROUND KNOWLEDGE

The project pathway encourages students to engage with the essential question by creating a product or project, often developing the skills of collaboration and teamwork.

STUDENT
Considers the Essential Question. Determines audience for project or product

TEACHER
Ties project to the Essential Question, introduces and reviews the project rubric with class

STUDENT
Gathers evidence, collects materials, plans, researches, writes

TEACHER
Directs students by modeling History-Social Science skills, such as extracting evidence, and provides any needed student support

ENGAGE

STUDENT
Listens and participates in teacher-led activity

TEACHER
Presents bell-ringer activity

TEACH & ASSESS

STUDENT
Reviews expository narrative, completes performance tasks, and checks for understanding

TEACHER
Lectures and/or leads discussion about main content in section

TEACH & ASSESS is repeated for each section within the lesson

CLOSE & REFLECT

STUDENT
Demonstrates understanding by completing assessment, writing an essay, and/or participating in wrap-up activities

TEACHER
Evaluates data from student assessment or activity to guide instruction and differentiation

EVALUATE EVIDENCE & DRAW CONCLUSIONS

TAKE ACTION

STUDENT
Reports findings, organizes evidence, and produces a written statement or a discussion point

TEACHER
Enables student learning by presenting rubrics and student examples and grades student work

STUDENT
Based on research and position, student creates a plan to take real-world action on the topic

TEACHER
Directs students with some examples of action to take

CREATE THE PROJECT

DELIVER A PROJECT/PRODUCT

REFLECT ON & EVALUATE THE PROJECT

STUDENT
Assigns roles, divides work, works together to create a project, and evaluates group members' contributions

STUDENT
Delivers a project or a product that demonstrates their understanding

STUDENT
Uses rubrics for peer assessment, or self-assessment, evaluates process, revisits the question, makes connections to today

TEACHER
Connects project to relevance for today

Collaboration & Teamwork

PERFORMANCE ASSESSMENT STRATEGIES: PROJECT-BASED LEARNING

In response to the growing demand for accountability in the classroom, educators must use multiple assessment measures to accurately gauge student performance. In addition to quizzes, tests, essay exams, and standardized tests, assessment incorporates a variety of performance-based measures, such as project-based learning.

Project-based learning is a way of teaching and learning in which students apply and acquire knowledge, and develop skills by investigating complex questions or challenges over an extended period of time. Students use their creativity and collaboration skills to communicate their ideas. These activities help students become aware of diverse audiences for their work. Project-based learning includes individual products, group products, or a combination of both.

Teachers may allow students to choose the type of project to complete so that the project is more meaningful to them. McGraw-Hill Education offers a Hands-On Chapter Project for every chapter. Examples of these activities

include creating a graphic novel, writing a magazine cover story, and writing and illustrating for a travel journal. In addition to these more traditional activities, McGraw-Hill Education also provides a Digital Hands-On Project for every chapter. These fun and challenging projects include creating online maps, podcasts, and virtual speaking avatars. Links, tutorials, and guides, other resources for each project are included. Chapter Inquiry Projects are included for every chapter.

What Are Some Typical Performance-Based Assessments?

There are many kinds of performance-based assessments. They all challenge students to create products that demonstrate what they know and their ability to apply it.

Writing

Performance-based writing assessments challenge students to apply their knowledge of social studies in a variety of contexts. Writing activities are most often completed by an individual rather than by a group.

✓ **Journals** Students write from the perspective of a historical character or a citizen of a particular historical era.

✓ **Letters** Students write a letter from one historical figure to another or from a historical figure to a family member or another audience.

✓ **Position Papers or Editorials** Students explain a controversial issue and present their own opinion and recommendations, supported with strong evidence and convincing reasons.

✓ **News articles** Students write a variety of stories from the perspective of a reporter living in a particular historical time period. This could also involve writing letters to the editor.

✓ **Biographies and Autobiographies** Students write about historical figures either from the third person point of view (biography) or from the first person (autobiography).

✓ **Creative Stories** Students integrate historical events into a piece of fiction, incorporating the customs, language, and geography of the period.

✓ **Poems and Songs** Students follow the conventions of a particular type of song or poem as they tell about a historical event or person.

✓ **Research Reports** Students synthesize information from a variety of sources into a well-developed research report.

Oral Presentations

Oral presentations allow students to demonstrate their social studies literacy before an audience. Oral presentations are often group efforts, although this need not be the case.

✓ **Simulations** Students hold simulations, or reenactments, of actual events, such as trials, acts of civil disobedience, battles, speeches, and so forth.

✓ **Debates** Students debate opposing viewpoints of a historical policy or issue. Students can debate from a contemporary perspective or in a role in which they assume a viewpoint held by a historical character.

✓ **Interviews** Students conduct a mock interview of a historical character or bystander.

✓ **Oral Reports** Students present the results of research efforts in a lively oral report. This report may be accompanied by visuals.

✓ **Skits and Plays** Students use historical events as the basis for a play or skit. Details should accurately reflect customs and the setting of the period.

Visual Presentations

Visual presentations allow students to demonstrate their social studies understandings in a variety of visual formats. Visual presentations can be either group or individual projects.

✓ **Models** Students make models to demonstrate or represent a process, place, event, battle, artifact, or custom.

✓ **Museum Exhibit** Students create a rich display of material around a topic. Typical displays might include models, illustrations, photographs, videos, writings, and audiotaped explanations.

✓ **Graphs or Charts** Students analyze and represent historical data in a line graph, bar graph, table, or other chart format.

✓ **Drawings** Students represent or interpret a historical event or period through illustration, including political cartoons.

✓ **Posters and Murals** Posters and murals may include maps, time lines, diagrams, illustrations, photographs, collages, and written explanations that reflect students' understandings of historical information.

✓ **Quilts** Students sew or draw a design for a patchwork quilt that shows a variety of perspectives, events, or issues related to a key topic.

✓ **Videos** Students film a video to show historical fiction or to preserve a simulation of a historical event.

✓ **Multimedia Presentations or Slide Shows** Students create a computer-generated multimedia presentation containing historical information and analysis.

How Are Performance Assessments Scored?

There are a variety of ways used to evaluate performance tasks. Some or all of the following methods may be used.

✓ **Scoring Rubrics** A scoring rubric is a set of guidelines for assessing the quality of a process and/or product. It establishes criteria used to distinguish acceptable responses from unacceptable ones, generally along a scale from excellent to poor. Rubrics clearly outline expectations for behaviors and outcomes. Rubrics may be used as guidelines as the students prepare their products. They are also commonly used for self-assessment.

✓ **Models of Excellent Work** Teacher-selected models of excellent work concretely illustrate expectations and help students set goals for their own projects.

✓ **Student Self-Assessment** Students can assess themselves using a variety of methods. Students can rank their work in relation to the model, use a scoring rubric, and write their own goals. Students can then evaluate how well they have met the goals they set for themselves. Regardless of which method or methods students use, they should be encouraged to evaluate their behaviors and processes, as well as the finished product.

✓ **Peer or Audience Assessment** Many of the performance tasks target an audience other than the classroom teacher. If possible, an audience of peers should give feedback to the student or group. Have the class create rubrics for specific projects together.

✓ **Observation** As students carry out their performance tasks, you may want to formally observe students at work. Start by developing a checklist, identifying all the specific behaviors and understandings you expect students to demonstrate. Then observe students as they carry out performance tasks, and check off the behaviors as you observe them.

✓ **Interviews** As a form of ongoing assessment, you may want to conduct interviews with students, asking them to analyze, explain, and assess their participation in performance tasks.

Hands-On History Chapter Project

Creating a Nation, From Beginnings to 1860

The Rise of a Nation

ESSENTIAL QUESTIONS
- *What characteristics define a society?*
- *Why do people form governments?*
- *How should societies settle disputes?*

Step 1: Researching Conditions in North America Students will use chapter lessons and do library or online research to create maps, tables, governing documents, and pamphlets for a new North American nation.

Directions Organize students into small groups. Have them assume the role of English people living around 1600. Each group of students will explore what area of North America is most likely to sustain a colony. Students should first make a list of criteria for a successful colony. For example, a colony will need a source of freshwater, timber for building, food sources, to be in a defensible location, to have a good harbor, and so on. Students should also research the locations and cultures of Native Americans living on the Atlantic coast. Next, students should create a map indicating the locations or availability of the resources on their list of criteria as well as any major landforms, such as mountains, rivers, or natural harbors. The map should also include the locations of Native American groups. Students should then determine the exact location for their colony.

Putting It Together Have representatives for each group share the chosen location with the class and summarize the benefits and challenges of settling in that location.

Step 2: Making Key Decisions Students will begin constructing a government based on what they have learned in Lesson 2.

Directions Tell students they are going to have a Constitutional Convention to determine the government of their new nation. First, have groups discuss the Constitutional Convention that gave rise to the U.S. Constitution. Groups should discuss how it was organized, what interests needed to be addressed, and how agreements and compromises were reached. Then, have the group decide on a plan for ratification of their Constitution—how will they, the convention, make final decisions on a plan? How will they present their plan to the citizens of their nation? Finally, have students decide on a basic structure for their government, including how power will be divided between branches of government, how citizens will participate in government, and how power will be divided between the federal government and the states. Students should then use their previously discussed process to "ratify" the constitution.

Hands-On History Chapter Project *Cont.*

Creating a Nation, From Beginnings to 1877

Putting It Together Ask each group to report on the choices they have made.

Step 3: Understanding the Significance of Reform Working in small groups, students will skim the chapter looking for the different reforms and reform movements that occurred in the United States during the early to mid-1800s and apply them to their young nations.

Directions Hold a class discussion in which you discuss the different reforms that occurred in the United States during the early to mid-1800s. On the board create a chart that has the headings: social, political, cultural, and economic reform. Have the students help you decide in which category to place each reform. Have each group choose which of the reforms or reform movements listed in the chart they feel would be most important for their own nation.

Putting It Together As reforms and reform movements are added to the chart, students should discuss the importance each has played in the history of the United States.

Step 4: Wrap-up This activity will synthesize the group's work over the course of the chapter by having them write a history of their nation.

Directions Have groups review their work, from their early research to their presentations on their nation's fictional civil war. Students will then write a coherent fictional history of their nation. Encourage them to use U.S. history as a model to show how a nation grows and sometimes divides and reunites.

Putting It Together Team members will collaboratively write their history, and then each member should write a short paragraph explaining how U.S. history served as an inspiration when writing their own nation's history.

Assessing Tell students that their presentation will be assessed based on these factors:

S: Student participates fully and actively in each group of which he or she is a member. Student contributes to all discussions and decision-making in both the smaller group and in the group as a whole. In all activities and research, student exhibits an excellent understanding of how to research and develop the multimedia presentation, of the steps needed in acquiring information and in how to build and present the presentation. Students demonstrate an understanding of how to best display the information and the content of the information does not show grammar flaws or sloppy, incomplete work.

T: Student participates in both the smaller group and the larger class. The student participates in the research and development of the presentation. Students show some understanding of the creation and the content in the presentation.

U: Student participates very little in the group and does little research. The student also has limited input into the research and development of the multimedia presentation that is created.

Hands-On History Chapter Project *Cont.*

Creating a Nation, From Beginnings to 1877

V: Student rarely participates in any groups, does incomplete and unsatisfactory research and development work, and offers little in the way of input to the rest of the group's needs. Student contributes little or nothing to the research and development of the presentation.

W: The student's work is unacceptable, with little or no participation in any aspect of the activity.

X: The student's work is poor, with no contributions to the group effort.

Technology Extension: Create a Colony using Google Docs

Google Docs is a free, collaborative tool that allows multiple writers simultaneously to contribute to and edit a shared document. With traditional computer programs, collaboration can be somewhat awkward, with multiple students hovering around a single computer or passing drafts with tracked changes back and forth. Google Docs allows multiple students to work simultaneously on the same shared document, creating a much richer opportunity for true collaboration. Through the utilization of online collaboration, learning becomes more student-centered, placing greater responsibility on the learner while increasing engagement, efficacy, and overall understanding of class content and concepts. Moreover, with Google Docs your students have the opportunity to co-create documents, presentations, spreadsheets, forms or drawings.

In this EdTechTeacher Technology Extension, we'll provide the resources to use Google Docs to encourage online student collaboration in researching, designing, and establishing a colony in North America.

Online Collaboration

Students can get access to Google Docs in two main ways. Many schools have Google Apps for Education accounts, where every student in the school is given an account with access to Gmail, Google Docs, Google Calendar, and other tools. If your school does not use this suite of services, you can have your student sign up for a regular Google account, which will then provide access to Google Docs and other Google services. Be sure to solicit the appropriate permissions in your school community before taking this step. With Google Docs, students can simultaneously write on documents and spread sheets, develop forms for collecting information, and work in partnership to produce presentations. Links to Web sites can be shared and discussed, and student feedback can be polled. Authorship is noted in a "history" section, so students and teachers can find out the contributions of individual students.

For more information regarding Google Docs, visit EdTechTeacher's Teaching History with Technology site: http://thwt.org/googledocs.html. Here, you'll find links to exemplars, tutorials for utilization, and suggestions and lesson plans for online collaboration as a part of the history classroom.

Using Google Docs to Establish a North American Colony

Face-to-face collaboration is an essential skill that all students should develop, and therefore be kept in place from the Hands-On Chapter Project. However, with online collaboration the teamwork can extend outside the class period and go on asynchronously, allowing students more flexibility in their contribution to the project. Furthermore, these tools allow for groups to easily edit their content before and after they have presented their maps, tables, governing documents, and pamphlets to classmates.

Teachers should familiarize themselves with Google Docs before assigning the use of the platform in researching, designing, and establishing their colony. Some class time should be spent modeling the platform and allowing students to begin experimenting with the different types of Google Docs.

There are two good ways to begin a Google Docs project. As a teacher, you can create unique blank project documents for each group and then invite all of the members of each group to be editors of the document. This is extra logistical work for you as a teacher, but it ensures that everyone is added to the correct documents and that you have editorial access to all of them. Alternatively, you can assign a leader to every group, and you can make this student responsible for starting documents, inviting all of the other group members, and inviting you to be an editor of the document. Once students have some familiarity with Google Documents, this is certainly the preferable way to begin a project.

Students should begin each step of the project by opening a new Google Doc that will best support their achievement of the desired outcome. Students can choose from documents, spreadsheets, presentations, forms, and drawings to collaboratively research and aid in designing their maps, tables, governing documents, pamphlets, and final summaries. While students may choose to make their pamphlets and maps by hand, Google Docs can offer foundational structure and help make their learning process visible for all.

Once each step of the project has been completed, they can be uploaded to a single repository, such as the class Web site, a blog, or wiki for students to examine and comment on before or after presentation in class. Remember, these documents are "living" so they can be updated and viewed at any time.

For more ideas about collaborating, visit the THWT collaboration page at http://thwt.org/discussion-collaboration/.

Assessment and Rubrics

You can assess the outcomes of each step in the project and create additional evaluation categories for their use of the Google Docs. Also, you may choose to measure how well students collaborate and provide comments to classmates. For more information about creating and modifying rubrics, visit http://thwt.org/rubrics.html.

Additional Online Resources

Further Resources: For additional resources on the Colonial Era, visit the following pages on the Best of History Websites. American History: Colonial page: http://besthistorysites.net/american-history/colonial/ American History: Pre-Colonial page: http://besthistorysites.net/american-history/pre-colonial/

Hands-On History Chapter Project

War and the West, 1844–1890

Making the Move West

Step 1: Planning Your Move Pairs of students will make a list of items to take with them as they prepare to move to the Great Plains to begin a new farm.

ESSENTIAL QUESTION

- *Why would people take on the challenge of life in the West?*

Directions Write the Essential Question on the board and ask pairs of students to assume the role of small farmers living in upstate New York. They have decided to sell their farm to seek new opportunities on the Great Plains. First, each pair of students should use the maps in this chapter, as well as library or Internet resources, to determine exactly where they will move. Have students create a list of "pros" and "cons" for the locations they're considering to help them make their decision. Remind students to consider the climate and geography of the region. Students should also plan what type or types of transportation they will need to get to their new farm, and at what cities and towns they will stop as they move west. After each pair of students has made their decisions, they should plot their route on an outline map of the United States, labeling the cities and towns along the way and the distances between each place.

Putting It Together Allow time for pairs to share their decisions and what they have learned about their destination as well as the places along their route. Students may also include pictures of the places where they will stop along the way.

Step 2: Preparing for the Trip Pairs of students continue to plan their trip west to begin a new farm on the Great Plains.

Directions Write the Essential Question on the board. Tell the pairs of students that they will make a list of the items they will need to take with them as they move west. Based on the information in the text, as well as library and Internet sources, students should first identify the items needed for survival—the bare necessities—in the Great Plains. Remind students to consider what resources they might find in their new locale as well as weather conditions. Next have pairs review their chosen route and the methods of transportation they will use.

Putting It Together Ask volunteers to explain what they are going to pack and why. Next have pairs share what they have learned about the Essential Question while preparing for the trip.

Step 3: Taking the Trip Students will describe the various people they will likely meet on their journey west.

Hands-On History Chapter Project *Cont.*

War and the West, 1844–1890

Directions Write the Essential Question on the board. Have the pairs of students refer to the map they created in Step 1. Using information from the textbook, as well as library or Internet resources, students should research the types of people they will likely encounter on their trip west. For example, as they move through towns and cities, they might meet merchants, innkeepers, and bankers. As they pass through established farmland, they might meet other small farmers. Finally, as they approach their destination, they might encounter native peoples. Based on their research, students should create brief personal profiles of five different individuals that they will likely meet along the way. Remind pairs to provide a physical description of the people, identify their occupations, and describe their daily lives. Students should also include how they interacted with each of the five people they profiled.

Putting It Together Ask volunteers to describe the people they have met on their journey west.

Step 4: Describing the Trip Students will synthesize what they have learned in Steps 1, 2, and 3.

Directions Write the Essential Question on the board. Have students refer to their maps, their lists, and the personal profiles of the people they encountered on the trip west. Using this information and what they have learned, students should write a brief paragraph describing the most difficult part of moving west and speculating as to why that difficulty might be worth overcoming. Ask volunteers to share their observations and list them on the board. Discuss their thoughts and observations.

Putting It Together Next, have students write a letter to a neighbor left behind in upstate New York. Students should use this letter to summarize the previous steps of the activity. They should describe how they decided where to move, what items they took with them, what route they traveled, and who they met along the way. Students should also describe difficulties they encountered along the way. Finally, they should conclude their letter by either recommending that their neighbor should join them on the Great Plains or recommending that their neighbor stay in upstate New York.

Assessing Tell students that their presentation will be assessed based on these factors:

S: Student participates fully and actively in each group of which he or she is a member. Student contributes to all discussions and decision-making in both the smaller group and in the group as a whole. In all activities and research, student exhibits an excellent understanding of how to research and develop the multimedia presentation, of the steps needed in acquiring information and in how to build and present the presentation. Students demonstrate an understanding of how to best display the information and the content of the information does not show grammar flaws or sloppy, incomplete work.T: Student participates in both the smaller group and the larger class. The student participates in the research and development of the presentation. Students show some understanding of the creation and the content in the presentation.

Hands-On History Chapter Project *Cont.*

War and the West, 1844–1890

U: Student participates very little in the group and does little research. The student also has limited input into the research and development of the multimedia presentation that is created.

V: Student rarely participates in any groups, does incomplete and unsatisfactory research and development work, and offers little in the way of input to the rest of the group's needs. Student contributes little or nothing to the research and development of the presentation.

W: The student's work is unacceptable, with little or no participation in any aspect of the activity.

X: The student's work is poor, with no contributions to the group effort.

Technology Extension: Westward Expansion Cell Phone Audio Journal

Cell phones and personal media devices are nearly ubiquitous in your classroom, but you may not have considered integrating them into your learning activities. Because your students already possess these items, little time needs to be spent learning the technology, and the projects can be implemented in or out of the classroom with ease and without added expense.

In this EdTechTeacher Technology Extension, we will show you how your students can use their cell phones and/or personal media devices to record an audio journal describing their journeys westward. This activity can serve as a replacement or an enhancement to the Hands-On Chapter Project.

Creating Audio Journals

Your students' cell phones or media devices will need to be capable of recording and processing digital audio. Many of today's Smartphones and personal music players already have a voice memo application. Free third-party apps are also a choice for students to download if their phones do not come with this technology. Most students are very familiar with the limits and capabilities of their devices. If your students do not have access to a personal cell phone or media device, you may choose to partner students or to allow students to record using a laptop computer instead. For more information about using cell phones and other handheld media devices in your classroom, visit the Teaching History with Technology Mobile Devices page at: http://thwt.org/mobile/mobile/. On this page you will find sample projects, links and tips, as well as video tutorials related to cell phones in the classroom.

You will need to set up a procedure for students to submit their work, either through e-mail, a classroom wiki or digital drop box, or another method of your choosing. Be sure to practice all steps of the project in order to anticipate student questions and familiarize yourself with the process.

Creating a Westward Expansion Cell Phone Audio Journal

Begin the project by completing steps 1-4 as outlined in the Hands-On Project. However, you should introduce the audio journal component at the outset so that students can begin their mental planning.

Activate background knowledge by playing an audio clip (or reading aloud) from a diary kept by a real pioneer who migrated west during the 19th century. A Web search should reveal several full text examples. The Oregon Trail Web Site, http://oregontrail101.com/, has many excellent examples.

Tell students that many people kept diaries of their journeys to record the scenery, terrain, their family memories, emotions, accomplishments, and trials, both for personal use and to share with others. Remind students that diaries would have been kept with pen and ink, but that 21st century devices such as cell phones and handheld media players would have enabled pioneers to record events while they walked. Tell your students that they will record a series of audio journal entries that could have been spoken by their pioneer personas. You can adjust the content and length specifications to fit your students' needs, but here is an example of guidelines for the audio journal.

Journal Entry 1	Journal Entry 2	Journal Entry 3	Journal Entry 4	Journal Entry 5
• Date • Location should be near the start of the trail • Introduce self and reasons for travel	• Date • Location should fit between start and middle of trail • Provide a detailed list of the items chosen to take on the journey and rationale for their inclusion	• Date • Location should be near the middle of the trail • Discuss the land that has been covered, including geography, climate and mileage	• Date • Location should fit between middle and end of the trail • Describe encounters with other people (Native Americans, immigrant settlers, merchants etc.)	• Date • Location should be the end of the trail • Reflect on the value of the journey, highs and lows, hopes for the future
Length: 1.5–2.5 minutes	Length: 2–3 minutes	Length: 3–4 minutes	Length: 3–4 minutes	Length: 4–5 minutes

While it is a good idea to use steps 1-4 in their planning, you may want students to avoid writing scripts so that these journals are conversational and informal in style. Students can always re-record if they need to, but they do not want their journals to seem rehearsed. Set guidelines for use of slang and vernacular of the time period. You may wish to give students a vocabulary list of words to use to build their journals for added support.

When students have finished their audio journals, they can e-mail them to you or upload them to a classroom wiki or file-sharing site. If time permits, you may want students to choose their favorite one to share with the class.

Assessment and Rubrics

You may wish to include categories related to length, clarity, and content evaluation. You may also choose to create a peer editing form for students to use to critique each other's work. For more information on building rubrics, go to http://thwt.org/rubrics.html.

Additional Online Resources

For more information about this time period, visit the Best of History Web Sites American History: Westward Expansion page at http://besthistorysites.net/american-history/westward-expansion/.

Hands-On History Chapter Project

Creating a Modern America, 1865–1901

Starting a Business

Step 1: Planning Your Business Working in small groups, students will determine what business they would like to start and how to organize it to be successful.

ESSENTIAL QUESTIONS
- *How did the United States become an industrialized society after the Civil War?*
- *Why do people migrate?*
- *How is urban life different from rural life?*

Directions Organize students into small groups. Have them assume the role of entrepreneurs. Using information from the chapter as well as library or Internet resources, each group of students should first determine what their business will be. Students should then make a list of the resources they will need for their business. Remind students to consider labor or human resources, natural resources, and financial resources, as well as machinery, factories, processing plants, and so on. Using library or Internet resources, students should determine how much capital will be needed to acquire the resources the group identified. Next, students should create a flowchart illustrating the processes that will likely be followed in their business. The flowchart should identify where in the process each resource identified by the group will be utilized or consumed.

Putting It Together Allow time for groups to share their decisions, what they have learned about their businesses, and the costs of the businesses. Students may also include pictures of the resources or of the processes used in the business.

Step 2: Obtaining the Capital

Directions Returning to their groups, students should review the plans, lists, and flowcharts for their business. Using their textbook as well as library or Internet resources, students should find out how business leaders obtain the money necessary to start a business. Remind students that a sole proprietorship is usually a small business owned by one person and that a partnership is owned by two or more people who usually invest their own money in the business. Larger businesses, however, require huge amounts of money, or capital. Two of the most common ways businesses obtain the large amounts of capital required are bank loans and the selling of stocks to investors, who then own part of the business. Each group should prepare a chart showing the advantages and disadvantages of these two options. After the charts are complete, a representative from each group should share the group's chart and findings with the class. Next, have students return to their groups and decide the best way for their business to obtain the needed capital.

Hands-On History Chapter Project *Cont.*

Creating a Modern America, 1865–1901

Putting It Together Have volunteers from each group explain how the group plans to obtain the required capital and why the group chose that particular option. Discuss with the class the likelihood of each business's success in obtaining the necessary capital.

Step 3: Expanding the Business

Directions Returning to their groups, students should review the plans, lists, and flowcharts for their business. They should also assume that they have received the necessary capital and that, so far, their business is successful. Given their business's success, each group of business leaders now wants to expand the business by becoming more efficient, keeping costs low, and eliminating competition. Using their textbook as well as library or Internet resources, students in each group should research what steps might be taken to expand or improve the business. For example, the group might decide that vertical or horizontal integration might be a useful way to expand the business. Alternatively, the group may decide to expand the business by building more factories and hiring more workers. Each group should make a final recommendation based on members' research.

Putting It Together Have volunteers from each group present the group's recommendation to the class. Discuss with the class the pros and cons of the various recommendations. Have the class hypothesize which recommendations are likely to be the most successful.

Step 4: Working With a Union

Directions Have students return to their groups. Each group should assume that their business is successful and that the business owners are making a good profit. The business's workers have joined a union and are now asking for improvements such as better benefits, a shorter work week, and higher wages. Using their textbook as well as library or Internet resources, have each group make a list of their workers' specific demands. Groups should include a rationale from the workers' viewpoint for each request. Next, each group should review and evaluate the list of the workers' demands and determine how the business will work with the union to pay fair wages and create a safe and fair workspace. Remind the groups that each demand will likely cost money, thus reducing the profitability of the business or threatening its ability to employ as many workers. The group should provide a rationale for each of the business's decisions.

Putting It Together Have a volunteer from each group present to the class the list of workers' demands and the business's responses. Discuss what might happen if an agreement between the business and the workers cannot be reached. After the class discussion, groups may want to reconvene to reevaluate the business's decisions.

Step 5: Being an Entrepreneur Students will synthesize what they have learned in Steps 1, 2, 3, and 4.

Directions Have the groups of students review their business, its cost, its growth, and its relationship with its workers. Have students determine which of the general aspects of starting the business was the most difficult. Have each group try to reach a consensus. Have a volunteer from each group share the group's decision with the class. Discuss with students the challenges and rewards of entrepreneurship and industrialization in the United States.

Assessing Tell students that their presentation will be assessed based on these factors:

Hands-On History Chapter Project *Cont.*

Creating a Nation, From Beginnings to 1877

S: Student participates fully and actively in each group of which he or she is a member. Student contributes to all discussions and decision-making in both the smaller group and in the group as a whole. In all activities and research, student exhibits an excellent understanding of how to research and develop the multimedia presentation, of the steps needed in acquiring information and in how to build and present the presentation. Students demonstrate an understanding of how to best display the information and the content of the information does not show grammar flaws or sloppy, incomplete work.

T: Student participates in both the smaller group and the larger class. The student participates in the research and development of the presentation. Students show some understanding of the creation and the content in the presentation.

U: Student participates very little in the group and does little research. The student also has limited input into the research and development of the multimedia presentation that is created.

V: Student rarely participates in any groups, does incomplete and unsatisfactory research and development work, and offers little in the way of input to the rest of the group's needs. Student contributes little or nothing to the research and development of the presentation.

W: The student's work is unacceptable, with little or no participation in any aspect of the activity.

X: The student's work is poor, with no contributions to the group effort.

Technology Extension: Online Mindmapping

Mindmapping, sometimes called concept mapping, has been used by social studies teachers for years, allowing students to brainstorm, organize ideas, collect and present data, and determine relationships as they study historical concepts. For example, graphic organizers for recording notes and information are common forms of mindmaps. The proliferation of online mindmapping platforms provides students with an interactive and collaborative method of organizing concepts, details, and relationships. Most platforms allow mind maps to be exported electronically or printed for future use. Mindmaps differ from electronic presentations, as they do not have the same capability of integrating audio, video, or special effects.

There are various online platforms that allow teachers and students to mindmap. In this EdTechTeacher Technology Extension, we'll provide the resources that show you how to use these platforms to help your students create and collaborate with mindmaps.

Creating Online Mindmaps

As with most platforms, mindmapping programs offer a variety of different options for teachers and students. In order to create, save and export mindmaps, a current e-mail address is almost always required for logging into a platform. Online mindmaps are simple to create because text (and frequently images) can be manipulated, moved, tiered, connected, highlighted, and presented. Depending on the platform, students can share their ideas and content and collaborate asynchronously as they create mindmaps. Some mindmapping platforms require a subscription fee, but others are free or have discounts for educators.

For more information on creating and using mindmaps, visit the mindmapping page at EdTechTeacher's Teaching History with Technology site: http://www.thwt.org/mindmap.html. On this page you will find platforms for creating online mindmaps as well as tutorials.

Using Mindmaps to develop a business in Modern America

As students proceed through the steps of planning and expanding a business as outlined in the Hands-On Chapter Project, they can complement their work by creating mindmaps for many of the steps.

- For Step 1, student groups can create a collaborative map as they brainstorm the resources they will need for their business as well as develop a flowchart to illustrate the process of the development of their business.

- In Step 2, students can use the mindmapping platform to outline the advantages and disadvantages of raising capital by drawing bank loans and the selling of stocks to investors.

- Students can display, compare, and contrast horizontal and vertical integration in Step 3, adding notes to each method based on their research.

- Mindmaps can be used in Step 4 to organize the demands of workers, the rationale of the demands, their business' response to the demands, and their rationale for each response.

- The entire class can create a collaborative mindmap for Step 5 as they discuss the challenges and rewards of entrepreneurship and industrialization in the United States.

Assessment and Rubrics

To create a rubric to assess the mindmaps, visit the Rubric page at EdTechTeacher's Teaching History with Technology site: http://thwt.org/rubrics.html.

Additional Online Resources

Further Resources: For more Web sites, lesson plans, and activities related to late 19th century industrialism in the United States, visit the Gilded Age section of Best of History Web Sites: http://besthistorysites.net/american-history/the-gilded-age/.

Hands-On History Chapter Project

Becoming a World Power, 1872–1917

Preparing a Multimedia Presentation

Step 1: Research American Areas of Interest

ESSENTIAL QUESTION
- *How are empires built?*

Directions Divide the class into small groups, assigning each group one of the following countries: Cuba, China, Japan, the Philippines, Puerto Rico, and Guam. Have students use Internet and library resources, as well as their textbooks, to locate and analyze information about the reasons for and the effects of imperialism in their assigned country. Encourage students to use both primary and secondary resources in their research.

Putting It Together Give students a tutorial on the software they will be using to develop their presentations. Encourage students to ask questions about aspects of the program they find confusing. If necessary, pair students who have experience using the program with those who do not.

Step 2: Organizing Information on the Presentation Groups begin to create and organize their presentations.

Directions Have students meet in their groups with the notes they have taken on their assigned country. Have groups discuss how they want to organize the information they've gathered. Suggest the options of chronology, cause-and-effect, or organization by subcategory. Once groups have determined the format, have them begin assembling the information they want to include in their presentations. Encourage students to use primary source quotes, informational text, diagrams, photographs, or even drawings they've created. Students may also use propaganda from the period.

Putting It Together Have students review their presentation once they have entered their information to verify the accuracy of the information and to make sure nothing has been omitted.

Step 3: Editing the Presentation Groups will edit their presentations for accuracy, content, and mechanics.

Directions Have groups run through their presentations to make sure that links to other pages are working properly and that all information is displayed correctly. Students should also edit their presentations for grammar, punctuation, and sentence structure. Encourage students to pair up with another group and review each other's presentations. Tell students that presentations should be coherent and easily understood.

Putting It Together Once students have reviewed their presentations, they should make any necessary changes, additions, or corrections.

Step 4: Sharing the Presentation Groups will share their presentations with the class.

Hands-On History Chapter Project *Cont.*

Becoming a World Power, 1872–1917

Directions Tell students to develop a narrative to go along with their presentations. The narrative should complement their presentations and explain the causes and effects of imperialism in their assigned nation. Once all groups have presented, encourage students to individually take a closer look at any of the presentations that intrigued them. Next have students critique the presentations on quality of information, ease of use, and creativity. Encourage students to share aspects of their own presentations they found interesting or challenging.

Putting It Together Have students discuss each of the six countries presented: Cuba, China, Japan, the Philippines, Puerto Rico, and Guam. Ask students to draw a conclusion about the effects of imperialism on other nations.

Assessing Tell students that their presentation will be assessed based on these factors:

S: Student participates fully and actively in each group of which he or she is a member. Student contributes to all discussions and decision-making in both the smaller group and in the group as a whole. In all activities and research, student exhibits an excellent understanding of how to research and develop the multimedia presentation, of the steps needed in acquiring information and in how to build and present the presentation. Students demonstrate an understanding of how to best display the information and the content of the information does not show grammar flaws or sloppy, incomplete work.

T: Student participates in both the smaller group and the larger class. The student participates in the research and development of the presentation. Students show some understanding of the creation and the content in the presentation.

U: Student participates very little in the group and does little research. The student also has limited input into the research and development of the multimedia presentation that is created.

V: Student rarely participates in any groups, does incomplete and unsatisfactory research and development work, and offers little in the way of input to the rest of the group's needs. Student contributes little or nothing to the research and development of the presentation.

W: The student's work is unacceptable, with little or no participation in any aspect of the activity.

X: The student's work is poor, with no contributions to the group effort.

Technology Extension: Online Multimedia Presentation on Imperialism

Crafting excellent multimedia presentations is an important academic and work skill for the 21st century learner. Multimedia presentations force students to think critically about the message they are presenting and enable idea linking, content revision, and dynamic choices for representing their understanding. In this EdTechTeacher Technology Extension, your students will prepare an online multimedia presentation after having analyzed research about their chosen country. Students will collaborate to creatively design slide shows that capture the reasons for and the effects of imperialism in their countries by using text, images, audio, video, and drawings. Once completed you can share your class presentations via e-mail, blog, Web site, wiki, or through slide-sharing sites.

Creating an Online Multimedia Presentation

There are many platforms for collaboratively creating online multimedia presentations. To learn more about creating and setting up this type of project, visit the Multimedia Presentations page at EdTechTeacher's Teaching History with Technology site: http://thwt.org/presentations.html. On this page you'll find an overview of multimedia presentation tools, examples of presentations, and other collaborative project ideas. As these tools are free, it is recommended that you familiarize yourself with the functionality prior to implementing it in class. You should also expect that students will learn features and techniques beyond what you show them.

A simple way to get started with this project is for you to set up a blank presentation for each group and then invite participants. It is recommended that you maintain editor access to each project so you can monitor activity throughout the process and make changes if necessary. Provide students viewer access to the other presentations in order to help idea sharing and knowledge building within the class.

Through open dialogue, early and often, students should plan how they will incorporate their research into their presentations. Multimedia presentation programs support multiple media formats so students can choose to include video and audio clips, images, text, and drawings in varying amounts as long as they accomplish the goals set out for them. Because the presentations are accessible from inside and outside of school, students can revise content at any time and work together to complete a product of the highest level.

Once they have completed their presentations you could import them into one class product or share them individually.

Create a Multimedia Presentation on Imperialism

Divide the class into small groups, assigning each group one of the following categories: Cuba, China, Japan, the Philippines, Puerto Rico, and Guam. Have your groups of students work collaboratively to create multimedia presentations about the reasons for and the effects of imperialism in their assigned country. Encourage students to use both primary and secondary resources in their research. Tell students to focus on the following causes and effects of imperialism: economics, naval power, national pride, Manifest Destiny, loss of autonomy, increased development, and war and other conflicts.

Provide students with an overview of the chosen online multimedia presentation tool by reviewing a sample presentation. Have students take notes in their presentations to familiarize themselves with the multimedia tool and create a lasting record of the discussion. When using an online collaborative presentation tool,

Copyright © McGraw-Hill Education. Permission is granted to reproduce for classroom use.

groups of students can create blank pages within their presentations to serve as a shared storehouse for their text, images, and video research. Task students with inputting different multimedia and recommend they share best practices between groups throughout the project.

Using the sample presentation, outline features of a successful slide and discuss pros and cons of your slides.

Because the online presentation tools allow for asynchronous work and 24/7 access, students can complete some of this work outside of school depending on their Internet access at home or afterschool.

Tell students to develop a narrative to go along with their presentations. The narrative should complement their presentations and explain the causes and effects of imperialism in their assigned nation. Depending on the tool you choose, this narrative could be prerecorded allowing the presentation to stand-alone.

Students should complete the design and themes of the presentations as a group during class time, so you are able to support their progress and offer advice. Have groups practice delivering their presentations to make sure that links to other pages are working properly and that all information is displayed correctly. Students should also edit their presentations for grammar, punctuation, and sentence structure. Encourage students to pair up with another group and review each other's presentations. Tell students that presentations should be coherent and easily understood.

Once all groups have presented, encourage students to individually take a closer look at the presentations that intrigued them. Next have students critique the presentations on quality of information, ease of use, and creativity. Depending on whether you share the presentations via e-mail, blog, Web site, wiki, or through slide-sharing sites, you can add comments at the published location.

Have students synthesize their learning by drawing conclusions about the effects of imperialism on other nations in a whole class discussion.

Assessment and Rubrics

To create a rubric to assess the multimedia presentation, visit the Rubric page at EdTechTeacher's Teaching History with Technology site: http://thwt.org/rubrics.html

Additional Online Resources

Further Resources: For more Web sites, lesson plans, and activities related to Imperialism, visit the Best of History Sites Page: http://besthistorysites.net/american-history/early-imperialism/

Citation Tools: To help students with their citation, you might encourage them to use one of several online citation generations. For more on these free, online tools, visit the Citation page at Teaching History with Technology: http://thwt.org/citation.html

Creative Commons: Creative Commons is a nonprofit organization that develops, supports, and stewards legal and technical infrastructure that maximizes digital creativity, sharing, and innovation. Aid students in navigating Internet searches for multimedia resources at Teaching History with Technology: http://thwt.org/creativecommons.html

Hands-On History Chapter Project

The Progressive Movement, 1890–1920

Learning How Government Affects People's Lives

ESSENTIAL QUESTION
- *Can politics fix social problems?*

Step 1: Becoming a Progressive In the first of four activities for this chapter, students will relate their knowledge of the problems that progressives addressed to contemporary community issues. They will identify a community problem and suggest a solution.

Materials: Student Edition

Directions Have students review Lesson 1, noting the types of issues that reformers tackled. Each student will then identify a problem in his or her community that affects citizens' lives today.

Identifying Problems and Solutions Students will either present to the class or write an analysis of the problem that includes these points: problem description, explanation of why they think the problem exists, and a statement about whether or how they believe government should go about solving the problem. If they believe the problem should not or cannot be solved by government, students should explain why and what other resources should be used.

Step 2: Create a Conservation Poster To reinforce the ways in which government's conservation efforts affect people's lives, each student will choose a conserved or preserved area of the country, such as Yellowstone National Park, the Florida Everglades, or the Arctic National Wildlife Refuge, and create an annotated poster. Their posters should present arguments for preservation or conservation and give examples of their chosen method in action.

Materials: Student Edition; access to an atlas or other maps in a library or on the Internet; poster board; unlined paper; pens, markers, or paints; scissors; paste

Directions Have students use library or Internet resources to trace, copy, or print a map of their chosen conserved area. They will then draw or paste pictures of the plant and animal life it protects, and any recreation it provides.

Analyzing Special-Purpose Maps In a box on the poster, students should add and complete these bulleted items: Date Conserved/Preserved, Reason for Conservation/Preservation (social or natural value), Conservation/Preservation Authority (legislation or other action that protected the area), and Recent Action (efforts to expand or develop the site, legal action, and so on). Display the posters in the classroom or somewhere else in the school.

Step 3: Presentations Students will work in groups to present the community problem they researched or their conservation posters.

Materials: Posters made in the previous step

Hands-On History Chapter Project *Cont.*

The Progressive Movement, 1890–1920

Directions Have students work together as a team to present a community problem and its resolution to the class. Students may also choose to present their conservation posters.

Representing Information Give students time to prepare for their presentations. They may role-play or use media other than their posters to present the information. Encourage students to state the topic clearly, describe it, and summarize the information.

Step 4: Wrap-Up This activity will synthesize the causes of the Progressive movement and its effects on people's lives by personalizing the issues.

Materials: Posters made in Step 2

Directions Divide the class into six teams. Each team should select one presenter to take on the role of an individual whose life was affected by the Progressive movement (such as a former child laborer now enrolled in school, a woman voting for the first time, and so on). To avoid duplication among the teams, have each team announce which role their presenter will play. If there are duplicates, assign another role to one of the teams. Be sure at least one team covers the effects of progressivism on some aspect of business, society, and politics.

Analyzing Information Team members will collaboratively write a journal page from the perspective of the presenter. Each journal page should describe vividly the person's life before and after the reform resulting from progressives' efforts. It should also mention the legislation or other action that made the reform possible. Presenters will read the group's journal page to the class. The rest of the class may want to ask the presenters questions. To make the presentations more lively and memorable, presenters may wish to carry relevant signs, dress in costumes, or hold up photos.

Assessing Tell students they will be assessed based on these factors:

S: Student participates fully and actively in each group of which he or she is a member. Student contributes to all discussions and decision-making in both the smaller group and in the group as a whole. In all activities and research, student exhibits an excellent understanding of how to research and develop the multimedia presentation, of the steps needed in acquiring information and in how to build and present the presentation. Students demonstrate an understanding of how to best display the information and the content of the information does not show grammar flaws or sloppy, incomplete work.

T: Student participates in both the smaller group and the larger class. The student participates in the research and development of the presentation. Students show some understanding of the creation and the content in the presentation.

U: Student participates very little in the group and does little research. The student also has limited input into the research and development of the multimedia presentation that is created.

Hands-On History Chapter Project *Cont.*

The Progressive Movement, 1890–1920

V: Student rarely participates in any groups, does incomplete and unsatisfactory research and development work, and offers little in the way of input to the rest of the group's needs. Student contributes little or nothing to the research and development of the presentation.

W: The student's work is unacceptable, with little or no participation in any aspect of the activity.

X: The student's work is poor, with no contributions to the group effort.

Technology Extension: Learning How Government Affects People's Lives Social Networking Pages

The Progressive Era was a period of awareness of social, political, economic, and environmental issues in the United States during the later 19th and early 20th centuries. During this period, the first national parks were created, as were laws regulating trusts, child labor and workers' rights, among other issues.

By allowing students to develop pseudo-"social networking" pages on various topics relevant to the Progressive Era, they research and learn about issues, conditions and reforms of the times. Students can share information and thoughts on each other's pages thereby enriching understanding of the period.

Creating Social Network pages

To learn more about social networking in the classroom, visit the Social Network page at EdTechTeacher's Teaching History with Technology site: http://www.thwt.org/socialnetwork.html. On this page, you will find extensive background information on social networking, including tips, tricks, links, and other sample activities.

As the teacher will note, there are several available "classroom friendly" social networking sites. However, the teacher should review in advance school and school district policies regarding use of social networking tools in the classroom. Also, the teacher should visit sites to be used prior to beginning the lesson to ensure those sites are available and not blocked by a school filtering system.

Creating Learning How Government Affects People's Lives Social Networking Pages

Students will proceed with steps 1 through 4 as outlined in the project overview, but should be informed that their presentations will be developed as social networking pages rather than by writing traditional journal pages. The teacher will want to modify the group task list on the Hands-On Chapter Project overview by having each of the six groups develop a social networking page, as well as find content for that page. The teacher should also ask student groups to post to each other group page their feelings and thoughts regarding that group's situation and whether they agree with reforms that help that group.

The teacher will want to follow this structure in conducting the project:

- **Step 1:** The teacher should ensure that students have a good background of the issues and crusades of the Progressive movement. If needed, students should review Lesson 1.

- **Step 2:** The teacher should divide the class into groups, and have each group create a "social networking" page focusing on the Progressive Era.

- **Step 3:** Inform the groups that they will act as "Progressive leaders," identify a current community issue or problem, and as a group, suggest a solution for that problem or issue. They should include an analysis of the problem on their social network page including the following points: description of the project, explanation of why the problem exists, a statement about whether or how they believe government should go about solving this problem. If they believe the problem cannot or should not be solved by government, the group should explain why and suggest what other resources can be used to solve the problem.

- **Step 4:** Groups will next look at the efforts of Progressives in the area of conservation of natural resources. The groups should select a conserved area of the United States, such as Yellowstone

National Park or a local area. Have the groups do online research for maps of the conserved area, and copy and paste the map onto their social network page. Students should also add the following information to their page, date the area was preserved, reason for preservation (the area's value to society), conservation authority (legislation or other action that protected the area), and recent action (efforts to expand or develop the site and legal action).

- **Step 5:** Each group should present information from their community problem or conservation social networking posts to the class. It would be helpful for the teacher to either allow class viewing of social networking pages using an LCD projector or some other method of projecting the pages.

- **Step 6:** Student groups should take the role of an individual whose life was affected by the Progressive movement. (for example, a former child laborer now enrolled in school, a woman voting for President for the first time, etc.) Have the group write an entry on their social network page that vividly describes their life before and after the legislation or action that made the reform possible. As with step 5, these posts should be made available to the class as a whole. Each group should select a "spokesperson" to role play the individual, or to provide photos on the social networking page of someone who represents that group.

Since a major feature of real social networking is social engagement, it is an important aspect of the project to have students "reply" to the other groups' pages. The teacher may wish to have students "debate" via social networking over these issues, by having students roleplay historical actors and post in character on other groups pages.

Assessment and Rubrics

For advice on creating a rubric to assess the development of social network pages, visit the Rubric page at EdTechTeacher's Teaching History with Technology site: http://thwt.org/rubrics.html.

Additional Online Resources

Further Resources: For more web sites, lesson plans, and activities related to the Progressive Era, visit the Best of History Websites Progressive Era page: http://besthistorysites.net/american-history/progressive-era/

Hands-On History Chapter Project

World War I and Its Aftermath, 1914–1920

Presenting World War I

Step 1: Presenting the United States's Entry into the War

ESSENTIAL QUESTION

- *Why do nations go to war?*

Directions Explain to students that they will create one to three multimedia slides or screens to explain why the United States entered World War I. Divide students into two teams. The first team should focus on the root causes of the war. The second team should focus on American neutrality and how and why it changed. (In both groups, further division might be made between those responsible for boiling down the literal explanation and those finding graphic/visual elements.) Each team should come up with several choices of media to use for the team's slides.

Putting It Together When the two teams meet to finalize the choices for the slides or screens, they will have to think critically to summarize these topics into a few slides.

Step 2: Presenting the Home Front at the Start of the War

Ask: What actions did the United States take to mobilize for the war?

Directions Explain to students that they will create one to three multimedia slides or screens to explain the actions the United States took to mobilize for war. Divide students into two teams. The first team should focus on the mobilization of the military. The second team should focus on the mobilization of industry and the workforce. (In both groups, further division might be made between those responsible for boiling down the literal explanation and those finding graphic/visual elements.)

Putting It Together When the two teams meet to finalize the media choices for the slides, they will determine how the selected slides demonstrate the preparations of the United States for war.

Step 3: Presenting the Battles and Victories of World War I

Ask: What were the crucial factors that led to a victory in the war?

Directions Explain to students that they will create one to three multimedia slides or screens to describe the factors that led to an Allied victory in the war. Divide students into two teams. The first team should focus on the battles and the factors that led to military victories. The second team should focus on the victory and the peace that followed. (In both groups, further division might be made between those responsible for boiling down the literal explanation and those finding graphic/visual elements.)

Putting It Together When the two teams meet to finalize the media choices for the slides, they will determine how to illustrate the battles of the war and the peace that followed.

Hands-On History Chapter Project *Cont.*

World War I and Its Aftermath, 1914–1920

Step 4: Postwar America

Ask: How did the war influence the economy and society of the United States?

Directions Explain to students that they will create one to three multimedia slides or screens to describe the effect of the war on the United States. Divide students into two teams. The first team should focus on the economy of postwar United States. The second team should focus on the American society after the war. (In both groups, further division might be made between those responsible for boiling down the literal explanation and those finding graphic/visual elements.)

Putting It Together When the two teams meet to finalize the media choices for the slides, they will determine not only how to illustrate the postwar economy and society, but also how to explain why the war had an impact on the economy and society.

Step 5: Wrap-Up Students will divide into teams to complete their presentations.

Directions Divide the class into two teams. Each team will complete the presentation by placing all the slides created in all lessons in this chapter into a unified presentation. Students will need to provide logical transitions between topics as well as edit the slides prior to presentation day.

Putting It Together Set aside class time for each team to give its presentation. Allow time for a discussion after all presentations have been given. Ask students the following questions:

- What were the main points of the presentation?

- Did the presentation present World War I clearly?

- Were the transitions clear?

- What were the good (and bad) parts of the presentation? How could it be improved?

Assessing Tell students that their presentation will be assessed based on these factors:

S: Student participates fully and actively in each group of which he or she is a member. Student contributes to all discussions and decision-making in both the smaller group and in the group as a whole. In all activities and research, student exhibits an excellent understanding of how to research and develop the multimedia presentation, of the steps needed in acquiring information and in how to build and present the presentation. Students demonstrate an understanding of how to best display the information and the content of the information does not show grammar flaws or sloppy, incomplete work.

T: Student participates in both the smaller group and the larger class. The student participates in the research and development of the presentation. Students show some understanding of the creation and the content in the presentation.

U: Student participates very little in the group and does little research. The student also has limited input into the research and development of the multimedia presentation that is created.

Hands-On History Chapter Project *Cont.*

World War I and Its Aftermath, 1914–1920

V: Student rarely participates in any groups, does incomplete and unsatisfactory research and development work, and offers little in the way of input to the rest of the group's needs. Student contributes little or nothing to the research and development of the presentation.

W: The student's work is unacceptable, with little or no participation in any aspect of the activity.

X: The student's work is poor, with no contributions to the group effort.

Technology Extension: WWI Polls and Cell Phone Classroom Response Systems

Classroom Response Systems (or clickers) are emerging as a fantastic way for teachers to elicit classroom participation during presentations, lectures, and activities. Classroom response systems allow teachers to create poll questions that students can respond to using a 'clicker' device that is part of a response system. However, access to classroom response systems are often an obstacle, as these systems are not readily available for every classroom teacher.

There are free online alternatives available to educators that allow students to participate and vote in classroom polls by utilizing their own cell phones and text messaging. By using these free cell phone alternatives to traditional classroom response systems, teachers can create poll questions to be used during a presentation or lecture that quickly checks student understanding. Students can also utilize cell phone polls to supplement their projects and presentations. In this EdTechTeacher Technology Extension, you will learn how to create, edit, manage, and use cell phone polls in class and then have your students incorporate cell phone polls into their World War I presentations.

Creating Polls with Cell Phone Classroom Response Systems

There are a number of free alternatives available to create cell phone polls. Most Web sites are quite similar and offer common features for cell phone polls. These features typically include:

- 30 cell phone votes per poll

- Poll questions can be saved, edited, and copied

- Poll results appear in real time (watch the results change as votes are cast)

- Poll results can be projected

- Unlimited number of poll questions

- Text message voting

- Poll restrictions (number of votes per cell phone can be adjusted)

Before using cell phone polls in your classroom, create an account and poll to practice voting with your own cell phone to get used to the voting process. To learn more about using cell phones as classroom response systems, visit the Mobile Devices page at EdTechTeacher's Teaching History with Technology site: http://thwt.org/mobile/mobile/.

On this site you will find tutorials, examples, classroom videos and resources to begin using cell phones as classroom response systems in your classroom.

To incorporate cell phone polls into student presentations, you can follow the Hands-On Chapter Project for World War I as it is described, but include an additional requirement for each step of the project that will require groups to create polling questions based on the content and slides that they have created for the Hands-On Project. The polling questions can be multiple choice type responses that focus on revealing student opinion about World War I.

For each step in the Hands-On Chapter Project, require the groups to create one poll question that will supplement the research and content that they have included in their slide.

The poll suggestions below can be used as a guide to get students started creating polls to supplement their presentations.

Step 1: The United States's Entry into the War

- Poll Suggestions:

  - What was the most significant cause of World War I?

  - Why did America move away from neutrality?

Step 2: The Home Front at the Start of the War

- Poll Suggestions:

  - What is the most difficult aspect of mobilizing a military?

  - Which industry best contributed to mobilizing the American military?

Step 3: Battles and Victories of World War I

- Poll Suggestions:

  - Why was the American military able to win numerous battles in World War I?

  - Which was the most significant American battle victory?

Step 4: Post-War America

- Poll Suggestions:

  - What effect did World War I have on the American economy?

  - Which aspect of American society changed the most after World War I?

Step 5: Class presentations with cell phone polls

- When each group is presenting their project to the class set up an LCD projector with a computer that has an Internet connection. Have students log into their cell phone polling account and project the cell phone polling question at the appropriate stage in their presentation.

Assessment and Rubrics

For advice on creating a rubric to assess the Hands-On Chapter Project and polling questions, visit the Rubric page at EdTechTeacher's Teaching History with Technology site: http://www.thwt.org/rubrics.html

Additional Online Resources

For additional resources visit the World War I page on EdTechTeacher's Best of History Sites: http://besthistorysites.net/american-history/wwi/

Hands-On History Chapter Project

The Jazz Age, 1921–1929

Creating a Memory Book

Step 1: Selecting Memorable Participants Students will skim the chapter and choose a person who played a role in the events of this chapter. Students may choose people mentioned in the chapter or research other people not mentioned, but involved in the events of this period. Students will learn more about him or her in order to contribute a page to a class memory book.

ESSENTIAL QUESTIONS

- *How was social and economic life different in the early twentieth century from that of the late nineteenth century?*
- *How has the cultural identity of the United States changed over time?*

Directions Make a scrapbook with the title "Memories of the Jazz Age" on the cover, and write the title on the board. Ask students to list on the board the names of people they may already know who played active roles in this period, such as Calvin Coolidge, Henry Ford, John T. Scopes, Mary Pickford, or Duke Ellington. Have students read ahead or do research to add as many names to the list as there are class members. Then have each student choose one name from the list.

Analyzing Information Students will identify the role played by each person added to the list.

Step 2: Researching Selected Names Each student will do research on the name chosen in Step 1.

Directions Have students use library, Internet, or family resources to learn more about the person whose name they chose. They should write a short biography of the person, and select a quotation or short paragraph written by the person, if possible.

Evaluating Information To decide which information to include, students will gain practice in evaluating the reliability of sources and the relevance of the information to the project.

Step 3: Researching Images for Selected Persons Ask students to gather photos and information about the person's background, motivation, and his or her role in the history of this period.

Ask: What is the goal of this interview? What information am I trying to get?

Directions Students will illustrate the biography of the person by finding photographs and related images or by drawing diagrams related to the person. Students should annotate all images with captions or explanations.

Hands-On History Chapter Project   *Cont.*

The Jazz Age, 1921–1929

Identifying Central Issues Students must identify the central role played by the selected person and illustrate the biography with images that relate to this role.

Step 4: Selecting and Researching a Cultural Innovation Ask students to choose a cultural innovation discussed in Lesson 4. Students will work in teams to design and create a memory page centered on the innovation selected.

Directions Have students either take turns stating their selected topic or write their topics on a class sheet of paper. Then have students divide into groups of two or three to create the memory page.

Analyzing Information Students will need to determine how to illustrate their topic using both images and text. Students will summarize the importance of the innovation through their page design.

Step 5: Design a Class Memory Page Students will collaborate as a class to plan, design, and create a memory page focused on the content of Lesson 5—African American Culture and Politics.

Directions Divide the class into four groups. Each group will sketch a storyboard that depicts, using both images and text, the African American culture of this historical period. After the groups have created their storyboards, bring the class into one discussion. Have group representatives present their ideas, and then decide on a class presentation of the topic. The class will then determine roles for each group to build the memory page.

Synthesizing Information Students will collect information from each group and determine the best way to present the topic using all the ideas presented.

Step 6: Wrap-Up Students will use their prior knowledge and the materials they researched to edit and revise the pages of the memory book.

Directions Give each student a page of the memory book. Each student will edit and revise the page as needed to create an attractive, informative page. They may wish to decorate the pages with other appropriate images, as well. The complete book may be used by the class to review the chapter and then displayed in the school.

Analyzing Information Students will determine the main topics presented and clarify the information to best represent the main ideas of the topic.

Assessing Tell students that their presentation will be assessed based on these factors:

S: Student participates fully and actively in each group of which he or she is a member. Student contributes to all discussions and decision-making in both the smaller group and in the group as a whole. In all activities and research, student exhibits an excellent understanding of how to research and develop the multimedia presentation, of the steps needed in acquiring information and in how to build and present the presentation. Students demonstrate an understanding of how to best display the information and the content of the information does not show grammar flaws or sloppy, incomplete work.

T: Student participates in both the smaller group and the larger class. The student participates in the research and development of the presentation. Students show some understanding of the creation and the content in the presentation.

Hands-On History Chapter Project *Cont.*

The Jazz Age, 1921–1929

U: Student participates very little in the group and does little research. The student also has limited input into the research and development of the multimedia presentation that is created.

V: Student rarely participates in any groups, does incomplete and unsatisfactory research and development work, and offers little in the way of input to the rest of the group's needs. Student contributes little or nothing to the research and development of the presentation.

W: The student's work is unacceptable, with little or no participation in any aspect of the activity.

X: The student's work is poor, with no contributions to the group effort.

Technology Extension: Virtual Scrapbook

Many people use photo storing and virtual scrapbook platforms to save, share, and document travels in their own lives, but the platforms also offer a creative method for presenting research about different locations around the country and world and at different times in history. Virtual scrapbooks are an excellent medium for students to present images and information of simulated trips to close or far off locations. These scrapbooks may include images, video, audio, hyperlinks, and other creative reactions from their "travels." Most virtual scrapbooks can be embedded in existing Web pages or wikis and can be shared via social networking services. Students can collaborate online and help create content material for their classmates as well.

There are various online platforms that allow users to create, publish, and share virtual scrapbooks. In this EdTechTeacher Technology Extension, we'll provide the resources that allow you learn how to use these platforms to help your students create a virtual scrapbook or memory book of the Jazz Age.

Creating Virtual Scrapbooks

As with most platforms, online scrapbook programs differ in the extent of what users can do and how they can develop their finished product. In most platforms, users log in using a valid e-mail address and are presented with a blank page for their work. Images are usually uploaded, so students should collect their image files in a common folder for organization and easy upload. Most platforms have "scrapbooking" functions like text bubbles, stickers, matting shapes, layouts, and backgrounds, and many offer themes for a single page or an entire book. Students should be cautioned about getting too caught up in the design details and losing focus on the historical content, and assessment rubrics should reflect the importance of content over style.

Most scrapbooking platforms are commercial in nature and offer the possibility of printing bound version of the product. Some do offer assistance for educators.

To learn more about these platforms and creating scrapbooks, visit the scrapbooks page at EdTechTeacher's Teaching History with Technology site: http://thwt.org/scrapbooks.html. On this page you'll find links to scrapbook platforms, an overview of creating scrapbooks, and examples of scrapbooks created by other classroom history teachers. If an online scrapbook program seems too detailed for students, an online eBook platform can be substituted. More information about eBook platforms can be found at the eBook page at EdTechTeacher's Teaching History with Technology site: http://thwt.org/ebooks.html.

Creating a Virtual Scrapbook for the Jazz Age

This project can be used as an extension for the Hands-On Chapter Project "Memories of the Jazz Age" scrapbook or as a substitution. Students should follow the same procedure in developing the project. Almost all scrapbook platforms require a login with an active e-mail account, and some allow teachers to create a class account for collaboration. Users can invite others to share on most platforms. Consult the various platforms in order to decide the approach to students logging in to the chosen platform.

Students should plan on creating a two page spread for their selected topic. The pages should contain a biography of an individual or a historical overview for the selected cultural innovation. Images, audio, video, and captions should be added to further explain the historical topic. Students should also pay attention to the "look" of the scrapbook page, selecting a theme, color scheme, and additional flourishes that apply to the topic. For example, two pages on Babe Ruth may incorporate a baseball theme, while a page on Clara Bow would have more of a cinema theme. Students should record the source of all images, which can be listed on the final page of the scrapbook or in a comments section.

The final scrapbooks can be collected and displayed through embedding or hyperlinks on a class Web site or wiki. In addition, the scrapbooks can be presented in class and used as the basis for a discussion about the Jazz Age.

Assessment and Rubrics

The project should be assessed based on historical content, use of visuals, and presentation and mechanics, and collaboration if required. For advice on creating a rubric to assess virtual scrapbooks, visit the Rubric page at EdTechTeacher's Teaching History with Technology site: http://thwt.org/rubrics.html.

Additional Online Resources

For more Web sites, lesson plans, and activities related to the Jazz Age, visit the Best of History Websites The Roaring 20s site: http://besthistorysites.net/american-history/the-roaring-20s/.

Hands-On History Chapter Project

The Great Depression Begins, 1929–1932

Making a Depression-Era Protest Sign (Sandwich Board)

Step 1: Finding Your Cause Have small groups work together to create protest or hunger march signs based upon Great Depression concerns.

ESSENTIAL QUESTIONS
- *What causes changes in the economy over time?*
- *How do depressions affect societies?*

Directions Divide the class into small groups. Tell students that many Americans chose to express their feelings about the economic conditions of the Great Depression through protests or hunger marches. Protests were held for many different reasons. Some protestors asked the government for help finding a job, others asked for farm aid, while some others asked for direct financial support. Have each group decide what they will protest or march in favor of. Students should refer to the chapter to brainstorm ideas for their protest signs.

Putting It Together Suggest that students divide the work according to their skills.

Step 2: Recording Your Messages

Directions Have students make their signs to reflect the condition they are protesting. Remind them to review the text to ensure their messages are as historically accurate as possible. Signs should be made to be as genuine as possible. Using era-specific language, materials, and construction will help achieve authenticity. Tell students to share in the work, as a family during the Great Depression may have worked on their signs together. Students will be asked to present their messages to the class in the next step.

Putting It Together Allow sufficient time for students to construct their signs. Remind students to look at the photos from the chapter to help create an accurate sign.

Step 3: Reviewing Your Work

Directions Each group should review their signs as a group, checking that the images and text are easy to understand and accurate. Tell students to remember the cause they decided on before creating their signs, and check that every element of the finished sign is appropriate for the message they wanted to express. If they decide to make changes, they can use correction tape, liquid paper, or cutting and pasting to edit their work.

Putting It Together Allow sufficient time for students to review their signs. Remind students that having a clear, strong message is the key to a good protest sign.

Step 4: Group Presentation

Directions Each group should present their sign to the rest of the class. Have the students explain what concern they chose to focus on with their sign. The messages on the signs should clearly communicate how students would have felt during the Great Depression.

Hands-On History Chapter Project *Cont.*

The Great Depression Begins, 1929–1932

Encourage the audience to offer feedback to each group. Comments should be constructive and helpful and should be limited to content, rather than focusing on the quality of the signs.

Putting It Together Have students review each group's sign. After each sign has been evaluated, have the students pick which sign best expresses a Depression-era concern.

Assessing Tell students that their presentation will be assessed based on these factors:

S: Student participates fully and actively in each group of which he or she is a member. Student contributes to all discussions and decision-making in both the smaller group and in the group as a whole. In all activities and research, student exhibits an excellent understanding of how to research and develop the multimedia presentation, of the steps needed in acquiring information and in how to build and present the presentation. Students demonstrate an understanding of how to best display the information and the content of the information does not show grammar flaws or sloppy, incomplete work.

T: Student participates in both the smaller group and the larger class. The student participates in the research and development of the presentation. Students show some understanding of the creation and the content in the presentation.

U: Student participates very little in the group and does little research. The student also has limited input into the research and development of the multimedia presentation that is created.

V: Student rarely participates in any groups, does incomplete and unsatisfactory research and development work, and offers little in the way of input to the rest of the group's needs. Student contributes little or nothing to the research and development of the presentation.

W: The student's work is unacceptable, with little or no participation in any aspect of the activity.

X: The student's work is poor, with no contributions to the group effort.

Technology Extension: Online Interactive Multimedia Posters

Posters allow students to present information in a visual medium by incorporating text, images, and color. By extending posters online, students can add multimedia (audio and video) and incorporate hyperlinks to additional Web sites that relate to their presentation topic. Interactivity makes the poster much more dynamic than a traditional two dimensional presentation. In addition, online multimedia posters can be viewed outside of the classroom setting, allowing students to create content for their classmates and extending learning beyond the classroom walls.

There are various online platforms that allow users to create multimedia posters. In this EdTechTeacher Learning Technology Extension, we will provide the resources that allow you learn how to use these platforms to create interactive multimedia posters.

Creating Online Interactive Multimedia Posters

As with most platforms, online multimedia poster programs differ slightly. In general, students develop a background, insert images and text, and determine their color scheme and layout. Some platforms allow for embedded audio and video and the incorporation of hyperlinks to other Web sites. For more information on creating online multimedia posters, visit the posters page at EdTechTeacher's Teaching History with Technology site: http://thwt.org/posters.html. On this page you will find links to various platforms, an overview of creating a multimedia poster, and an example of posters created by other classroom history teachers. Choose a platform that fits your students and assignment best.

Creating Multimedia Interactive Posters for a Depression Era Protest Sign

Students will need to join any of the multimedia poster sites by logging in with a username and an active email. It is always good practice for students to refrain from using their last name.

Students should create each multimedia Depression Era poster based on the procedure outlined in the Hands-On Chapter Project. Students should pay careful attention to the language, trying to replicate the vocabulary and the voice of the time. Protest posters should have images, colors, and fonts that fit with the era as well.

The multimedia potential of the online platforms allow for additional flourishes that can be added to the signs. Students can incorporate a Depression-era song that fits the mood of the sign by embedding music to add to the emotion of the sign. In addition, students can record primary source memories and embed them into the poster, adding a historical touch and authentic voice to the sign. If desired, students can also include hyperlinks to reliable Web sites about the era or specific topic.

Once the signs are completed, teachers can link all of the Depression posters in one online location for a virtual Depression protest meeting. The information can be discussed in a classroom setting or a processing assignment can be given as a reflection activity.

Assessment and Rubrics

The project should be assessed based on historical content, use of visuals, and presentation and mechanics, and collaboration if required. For more information about rubrics, visit the Rubric page at EdTechTeacher's Teaching History with Technology site: http://thwt.org/rubrics.html.

For more Web sites, lesson plans, and activities related to the Depression, visit the Great Depression section of Best of History Websites: http://besthistorysites.net/american-history/the-great-depression/

For other multimedia presentation tools, visit the THWT Presentations page at http://thwt.org/presentations.html.

Hands-On History Chapter Project

Roosevelt and the New Deal, 1933–1941

Publishing a Newspaper

ESSENTIAL QUESTIONS
- *Can the government fix the economy?*
- *Is government responsible for the economic well-being of its citizens?*

Step 1: Identifying U.S. Groups to Watch Small groups of students receive their assignments.

Directions Divide the class into five groups, assigning each group one of the following groups of Americans: women, children, African Americans, Native Americans, and Hispanic Americans. Tell students that they will create a newspaper from the viewpoint of their assigned group during the 1930s. The newspaper will include news stories, editorials, and cartoons. Encourage students to begin a separate section of their notebooks to take notes on the chapter from their assigned viewpoint and to record findings from additional research in the library or on the Internet.

Putting It Together Make sure that students have in-class access to copies of local and national newspapers as a model on which to base their own newspapers.

Step 2: Write and Plan Newspaper Copy Students begin to write articles and editorials and to draw cartoons based on the content of Lesson 1.

Directions Remind students to include the basic facts in news stories and to support opinions in editorials and letters to the editor. Have them plan the length of their newspaper and begin to write to fit that length. Encourage students to find templates online or in word-processing software that can help them place copy in newspaper format.

Putting It Together Invite a teacher familiar with word-processing programs to offer a tutorial for students unfamiliar with the software and how to use it.

Step 3: Copyedit and Content Edit the Paper Students submit their articles to designated "editors" who evaluate both the content and the grammar of the pieces.

Directions Ask each group to choose a person to be the editor. Then have groups exchange their articles so that an objective, outside reader sees each article. Then have students revise according to the feedback they receive.

Putting It Together Remind students that careful editing involves an attention to detail and to factual accuracy. Encourage editors to find positive comments to make about each piece they edit.

Hands-On History Chapter Project *Cont.*

Roosevelt and the New Deal, 1933–1941

Step 4: Produce and Distribute the Paper Have students make enough copies of their newspaper for the class. Allow time for students to read and comment on each other's completed work. Display the completed papers in the classroom.

Putting It Together Use the newspapers as the basis of a classroom display or bulletin board. Enhance the display with photos and maps.

Assessing Tell students that their presentation will be assessed based on these factors:

S: Student participates fully and actively in each group of which he or she is a member. Student contributes to all discussions and decision-making in both the smaller group and in the group as a whole. In all activities and research, student exhibits an excellent understanding of how to research and develop the multimedia presentation, of the steps needed in acquiring information and in how to build and present the presentation. Students demonstrate an understanding of how to best display the information and the content of the information does not show grammar flaws or sloppy, incomplete work.

T: Student participates in both the smaller group and the larger class. The student participates in the research and development of the presentation. Students show some understanding of the creation and the content in the presentation.

U: Student participates very little in the group and does little research. The student also has limited input into the research and development of the multimedia presentation that is created.

V: Student rarely participates in any groups, does incomplete and unsatisfactory research and development work, and offers little in the way of input to the rest of the group's needs. Student contributes little or nothing to the research and development of the presentation.

W: The student's work is unacceptable, with little or no participation in any aspect of the activity.

X: The student's work is poor, with no contributions to the group effort.

Technology Extension: Creating an eBook of New Deal Newspapers

As the world of education and instruction becomes increasingly reliant on technology, many teachers have utilized electronic books, or eBooks, in their classrooms. While eBooks serve as an excellent medium for students to receive content information once limited to the printed text, they also provide students with an exciting and dynamic publishing opportunity for work of their own. By producing eBooks, students can present their ideas as they would with traditional writing, but with added flourishes of embedded multimedia and hyperlinks. Students can help create content material for their classmates through electronic publishing as well.

There are numerous online platforms that allow users to create, publish, and share eBooks. In this EdTechTeacher Learning Technology Extension, we'll provide the resources that allow you learn how to use these platforms to help your students create and compile an eBook version of New Deal era newspapers.

Creating eBooks

As with most platforms, online eBook programs differ in the extent of what students can do and how they can develop electronic books. In most platforms, there are two possible methods of creating the electronic text and images. In one method, students create their content, including text and images, in a word processing program, save the document, and then upload the finished product into the eBook program for conversion. The advantages of this method include student familiarity with word processing programs and the associated tools of spelling and grammar check; however, some limits are placed on the finished product. The resulting eBook can usually be modified with the addition of links, multimedia, and dynamic elements, but the text and images stay the same as in the original document.

The other method involves creating and inserting all text, images, links, and multimedia directly in the eBook platform. This allows the student author much more freedom in creating the "look" of the eBook, including organization, visual appearance, and incorporation of multimedia and hyperlinks. The drawback is the necessity for an online connection at all times and an unfamiliar platform for most students.

For more information on creating eBooks, visit the eBooks page at EdTechTeacher's Teaching History with Technology site: http://thwt.org/ebooks.html. On this page you'll find links to various platforms, an overview of creating an eBook, and an example of eBooks created by other classroom history teachers.

Creating an eBook version of New Deal newspapers

Students will need to join any of the eBook sites by logging in with a username and an active e-mail. It is always good practice for students to refrain from using their last name. A group login can be developed as well for multiple students to collaborate in the same work. The New Deal newspaper eBook should follow the same model as outlined in the Hands-On Chapter Project. The individual newspapers should be completed on a word processing program. As stated in the project outline, newspaper templates can and should be utilized in order to develop a newspaper format. As students create their newspapers, they should make sure they are expressing the perspective of their assigned historical group. If students find audio or video that they feel will enhance their newspapers, they must consider where the embedded media will be placed in the finished newspaper. The newspapers should include a properly cited bibliography.

Once the individual newspapers are edited (for mechanics and content) and revised, they should be saved as .pdf files for importing into the eBook platform.

Once imported into the eBook platform, students should add multimedia. Students can add audio of primary source quotes (either actual historical audio or student narrated) for each event. Music from the era can be added to the eBook to provide a soundtrack for the images. Applicable historical or documentary clips can be embedded in the eBook as well. Essential hyperlinks for each event can be included for further enrichment for the reader.

The teacher can "collect" the completed newspapers and share them with and entire class by embedding them or providing links on a class Web site or wiki. The information can be discussed in a classroom setting or a processing assignment can be given as an extension activity.

Assessment and Rubrics

The project should be assessed based on historical content, use of visuals, and presentation and mechanics, and collaboration if required. For more information about rubrics, visit the Rubric page at EdTechTeacher's Teaching History with Technology site: http://thwt.org/rubrics.html.

Additional Online Resources

Further Resources: For more Web sites, lesson plans, and activities related to the New Deal era, visit the Great Depression section of Best of History Websites: http://besthistorysites.net/american-history/the-great-depression/.

Hands-On History Chapter Project

A World in Flames, 1931–1941

Creating a World War II Memory Book

ESSENTIAL QUESTION
- *Why do some people not respond to injustice while others try to prevent injustice?*

Step 1: Selecting Memorable People

Directions Ask students to list on the board the names of people who played a role in the war. Have students read ahead or do research to add as many names to the list as there are class members. Tell students to choose a name from the list and learn more about him or her in order to contribute a page to a class memory book. Have students use library, Internet, or family resources to learn more about the person whose name they chose. Ask students to gather photos and information about the person's background, motivation, and his or her role in the war. They should also select a quotation or short paragraph written by the person, if possible. Make a scrapbook with the title "Memories of World War II" on the cover.

Putting It Together Students will identify the role played by each person added to the list. When dictators are chosen, students will discuss what conditions in each country allowed the dictators to gain power.

Step 2: Debating the War Students will create a page in their memory book that documents the debate over whether the United States should remain neutral.

Directions Have students use library or Internet sources to find arguments for and against American neutrality in 1940. Students will build a page in the memory book that illustrates this debate.

Putting It Together Students will select quotations or summarize arguments for and against neutrality.

Step 3: Researching the Holocaust Students will work in groups to create a page in the memory book dedicated to Holocaust survivors.

Directions Have students use library, Internet, or family resources to learn more about the Holocaust and the survivors. Ask students to gather information about how they survived the war and lived their lives after the war. Students may choose to include primary sources on these pages of the memory book.

Putting It Together To decide which information to include, students will gain practice in finding relevant sources and synthesizing information from many sources.

Step 4: Wrap-Up Students will use their prior knowledge and the materials they researched to complete the pages of the memory book.

Hands-On History Chapter Project *Cont.*

A World in Flames, 1931–1941

Directions Give each student a page of the memory book and ask them to use the photos and information they researched to create an attractive, informative page. They may wish to decorate the pages with other appropriate images, as well. The complete book may be used by the class to review the chapter and then displayed in the school or donated to a local VFW chapter or other group.

Assessing Tell students that their presentation will be assessed based on these factors:

S: Student participates fully and actively in each group of which he or she is a member. Student contributes to all discussions and decision-making in both the smaller group and in the group as a whole. In all activities and research, student exhibits an excellent understanding of how to research and develop the multimedia presentation, of the steps needed in acquiring information and in how to build and present the presentation. Students demonstrate an understanding of how to best display the information and the content of the information does not show grammar flaws or sloppy, incomplete work.

T: Student participates in both the smaller group and the larger class. The student participates in the research and development of the presentation. Students show some understanding of the creation and the content in the presentation.

U: Student participates very little in the group and does little research. The student also has limited input into the research and development of the multimedia presentation that is created.

V: Student rarely participates in any groups, does incomplete and unsatisfactory research and development work, and offers little in the way of input to the rest of the group's needs. Student contributes little or nothing to the research and development of the presentation.

W: The student's work is unacceptable, with little or no participation in any aspect of the activity.

X: The student's work is poor, with no contributions to the group effort.

Technology Extension: Virtual Scrapbook

Many people use various photo storing and virtual scrapbook platforms to save, share, and document travels in their own lives, but these platforms also offer a creative method for presenting research about different locations around the country and world and at different times in history. Virtual scrapbooks are an excellent medium for students to present images and information of simulated trips to close or far off locations, including images, video, audio, hyperlinks, and creative reactions from their "travels." Most virtual scrapbooks can be embedded in existing Web pages or wikis and can be shared via social networking services. Students can collaborate online and help create content material for their classmates as well.

There are various online platforms that allow users to create, publish, and share virtual scrapbooks. In this EdTechTeacher Technology Extension, we will provide the resources that allow you learn how to use these platforms to help your students create a virtual scrapbook or memory book for World War II.

Creating Virtual Scrapbooks

As with most platforms, online scrapbook programs differ in the extent of what users can do and how they can develop their finished product. In most platforms, users log in using a valid e-mail address and are presented with a blank page for their work. Images are usually uploaded, so students should collect their image files in a common folder for organization and easy upload. Most platforms have "scrapbooking" functions like text bubbles, stickers, matting shapes, layouts and backgrounds, and many offer themes for a single page or an entire book. Students should be cautioned about getting too caught up in the design details and losing focus on the historical content, and assessment rubrics should reflect the importance of content over style.

Most scrapbooking platforms are commercial in nature and offer the possibility of printing bound version of the product. Some do offer assistance for educators.

To learn more about these platforms and creating scrapbooks, visit the scrapbooks page at EdTechTeacher's Teaching History with Technology site: http://thwt.org/scrapbooks.html. On this page you'll find links to scrapbook platforms, an overview of creating scrapbooks, and examples of scrapbooks created by other classroom history teachers. If an online scrapbook program seems too detailed for students, an online eBook platform can be substituted. More information about eBook platforms can be found at the eBook page at EdTechTeacher's Teaching History with Technology site: http://thwt.org/ebooks.html.

Creating a Virtual Scrapbook for World War II

This project can be used as an extension for the Hands-On Chapter Project "World War II Memory Book" or as a substitution. Students should follow the same procedure in developing the project. Almost all scrapbook platforms require a login with an active email account, and some allow teachers to create a class account for collaboration. Users can invite others to share on most platforms. Consult the various platforms in order to decide the approach to students logging in to the chosen platform.

Students should plan on creating a one page or two page spread for their selected topics. The "Memorable People" pages should contain a biographical overview, images, and quotes that explain the role played by then person during the war. The "Debating the War" page should successfully summarize the argument for or against neutrality, including essential quotations (typed, narrated, or historical audio). The "Researching the Holocaust" page can include actual audio and/or video interviews from survivors as well and images and text. Students should also pay attention to the "look" of the scrapbook page, selecting a theme, color scheme, and additional flourishes that apply to the topic. Citations should be included on the final page of the scrapbook or in a comments section.

The final scrapbooks can be collected and displayed through embedding or hyperlinks on a class Web site or wiki. In addition, the scrapbooks can be presented in class and used as the basis for a discussion about World War II.

Assessment and Rubrics

The project should be assessed based on historical content, use of visuals, and presentation and mechanics, and collaboration if required. For advice on creating a rubric to assess virtual scrapbooks, visit the Rubric page at EdTechTeacher's Teaching History with Technology site: http://thwt.org/rubrics.html.

Additional Online Resources

Further Resources: Web sites, lesson plans, and activities related to World War II, visit the Best of History Websites World War II site: http://besthistorysites.net/ww2/, including the World War II Special Topics site: http://besthistorysites.net/ww2/#special for information about the Holocaust.

Hands-On History Chapter Project

America and World War II, 1941–1945

An Interview with a Veteran

ESSENTIAL QUESTION
- *What kind of sacrifices does war require?*

Step 1: Finding a Veteran to Interview and Shaping the Questions

Directions Explain to students that they will document an interview with a veteran (using a CD or DVD). Students should begin by thinking about what they might learn from a veteran. For example, students could learn American attitudes in that person's community toward the war they were involved in, where he or she served, what he or she knew at the time about the country they served in, or how service affected his or her political views. The next and crucial task is to find a veteran to interview. A local Veterans of Foreign Wars group can be helpful (asking other community organizations or churches is also a possibility). Students may write a letter or phone the veteran to ask for his or her participation.

Putting It Together Once students know the basics about their interviewee (such as the branch of the military and the war involved), they should write out the questions they will ask in a question-and-answer format, organizing the questions in a logical fashion (the person's life before the war, mission during the war, and so on).

Step 2: Practicing the Interview

Ask: What is the most important information to get?

Directions Students should use the list of questions that they created in Step 1 to conduct mock interviews to get practice in interviewing (especially in being alert to follow up a question when a discussion gets off the script) and to help decide on the interviewing team. One to two students should be present at the interview. Students should select a location that is informal, yet quiet enough to conduct the interview without disturbances.

Putting It Together As students practice, they should refine their list of questions. Students should note the content of their questions. (Are they getting the information they want?) They should also note the length of their questions and question list. (Are there enough questions? Are there too many questions?) The interview should not take longer than one hour.

Step 3: Conducting the Interview

Ask: What is the goal of this interview? What information am I trying to get?

Directions Explain to students that only one or at most two people can actually meet with the subject (the second person may want to take notes). It is also a good idea to record the interview. Students should obtain permission from the subject to record. No more than one hour of the interviewee's time should be taken. The interview can be conducted in a home or at school (wherever a computer with a microphone hook-up is available).

Putting It Together After the interview, students should meet to review what happened and discuss it. Was anything missed? Are any answers ambiguous? Are there gaps in what the script had covered? This information will prepare students for Step 4.

Hands-On History Chapter Project *Cont.*

America and World War II, 1941–1945

Step 4: Editing and Presenting

Ask: What is the essential core of the interview to be preserved, and what introduction and conclusion needs to be added to it?

Directions Students will probably need to edit the material for the final product. They will also want to collectively write an introduction and conclusion for the final product. The tasks involved can be divided among the students according to their interests and skills. Then students should do a final edit of the interview by asking themselves:

- Did I give a good introduction?

- Are the questions and answers clear to my audience?

- What conclusions should be drawn from the information given?

- Did I close the interview with a summary or closing statement?

Set class time aside for students to present their interviews. Students may also present it to a community group and, certainly, to the veteran who was the subject.

Putting It Together Presenters should be prepared for follow-up questions from their audience. They should be sure that they have researched the topics covered in the interview and are familiar with those mentioned by the subject.

Step 5: Wrap-Up Students will review the presentations and provide an evaluation of their work.

Directions Students follow up their presentations with a self-evaluation of both the project and their work on it. Students should write a brief essay that answers the questions to the right.

- What was the most difficult part of this project? Why?

- What was the best part of this project? Why?

- What could be done to improve the presentation?

- What did I learn about war by completing this project?

Putting It Together Students should provide clear essays and succinct answers to each question above.

Assessing Tell students that their presentation will be assessed based on these factors:

S: Student participates fully and actively if part of an interview team. Student exhibits an excellent understanding of the techniques for researching, developing, and conducting an interview. Students will exhibit a strong sense of how to edit an interview, knowing and keeping the most relevant information, and how to build and present the final product in a presentation. Students demonstrate an understanding of how to best display the information and the content of the information does not show grammar flaws or sloppy, incomplete work.

Hands-On History Chapter Project *Cont.*

America and World War II, 1941–1945

T: Student participates in both the smaller group and the larger class. The student participates in the research and development of the presentation. Students show some understanding of the creation and the content in the presentation.

U: Student participates very little in the group and does little research. The student also has limited input into the research and development of the multimedia presentation that is created.

V: Student rarely participates in any groups, does incomplete and unsatisfactory research and development work, and offers little in the way of input to the rest of the group's needs. Student contributes little or nothing to the research and development of the presentation.

W: The student's work is unacceptable, with little or no participation in any aspect of the activity.

X: The student's work is poor, with little effort.

Technology Extension: Wiki Oral History Collection

With the development of various online platforms that allow users to publish original material in an assortment of formats, teachers and students have an incredible opportunity to collaborate and present content and opinion on the World Wide Web. Information can be conveyed through text, audio, video, art, images, or in any combination thereof. Teachers can present content in nearly countless formats, and students have an exciting and dynamic publishing opportunity for work of their own.

One such publishing method is a wiki. Wikis are terrific platforms for collecting and publishing a collection of oral history interviews. A wiki is a Web site where students can collaboratively create Web pages through an interface similar to a word processing program, an interface that does not require any special programming skills. In addition to text, wiki users can include images, audio, video, and embedded tools from other Web 2.0 platforms.

In this EdTechTeacher Technology Extension, we'll provide the resources that help you learn how to use a wiki to help your students create and compile an online collection of veterans' oral history.

Publishing Online

There are several wiki hosting services that allow K-12 teachers to set up wikis and subscribe their students as editors entirely for free. To learn more about creating and setting up wikis, visit the Collaborating with Wikis page at EdTechTeacher's Teaching History with Technology site: http://thwt.org/discussion-collaboration/wikis/. On this page you'll find an overview of using wikis, examples of wikis created by other classroom history teachers, links to wiki hosting platforms, and a series of video tutorials for creating and managing wikis.

Since creating wikis can be done freely, create a test wiki and play around with the features and settings before your create your "real" classroom museum project wiki.

Creating an Online Collection of Veterans' Oral History

Students should follow the Hands-On Chapter Project in order to research, develop, and conduct an interview with a veteran. Students can use online resources to locate local veterans' groups if necessary. They should think of the essential question for the chapter, "What kind of sacrifices does war require?", as they shape their questions and practice the interview.

Before conducting the interview, students should determine the eventual format of publishing the interview. They can easily chronicle the interview by using text, with the questions and responses written in longhand and transferred to text online or directly typed into the wiki or a word processing document. If audio or video are preferred, students will need to acquire the necessary hardware to successfully capture the interview. For audio recordings, students can use digital recorders, microphones on computers, or cell phones. Video can be captured with built-in webcams or handheld digital cameras.

Once the interviews have been conducted, teachers should create a wiki for the entire collection of interviews. A common login can be created for students, or individual students can create their own logins and be invited to collaborate. Students can then create individual pages for their interviews. Text-based interviews can be easily imported into the wiki, along with images. Audio and video can be uploaded to a site that allows file sharing and then embedded into the individual interview wiki page.

The final interviews should be presented to classmates, allowing for reflection and questions concerning the content and process. The benefit of collecting the interviews on an online wiki include having a chronicle of oral histories for future students to use, and also the ability to share the interviews with an unlimited audience—including all of the subjects who were interviewed.

Assessment and Rubrics

You can create evaluation categories for students' use of the multimedia features of wikis, their image selections, descriptions, collaboration, and analysis. One advantage of grading and assessing work completed on wikis is that wikis maintain a historical record of every edit made to every page (look on the "History" tab). These edit records allow you to gauge accurately how much each individual team member contributed to the overall project. For guidance on creating rubrics, see the Teaching History with Technology rubric page at http://thwt.org/rubrics.html.

Additional Online Resources

For more Web sites, lesson plans, and activities related to World War II, visit the Best of History Websites World War II site: http://besthistorysites.net/ww2/, including the World War II Special Topics site: http://besthistorysites.net/ww2/#special.

Hands-On History Chapter Project

The Cold War Begins, 1945–1960

Writing a Script to Demonstrate McCarthyism in Action

ESSENTIAL QUESTION

- *How did Cold War tensions affect American society?*

Step 1: Researching the Army-McCarthy Hearings of 1954

Directions Explain to small groups of students that they will be writing a script inspired by the Army-McCarthy hearings that were so influential, and which turned the tide against McCarthyism. For background, they can consult sources found online or in the library. Students can also research in books on McCarthy or McCarthyism to find direct quotations from the hearings or people who witnessed them.

Putting It Together Students should share their research and then discuss the essential elements they want to convey about McCarthyism in their script.

Step 2: Creating the Roles and the Script

Directions From reading about the hearings or even seeing them, if a historical video is available, students will create their script and cast different students in the lead and supporting roles. These roles should include Senator McCarthy, army lawyer Joseph Welch, other senators on the committee, and a witness. Students will determine a reasonable length for the script and how to divide writing responsibilities ensuring full group participation.

Putting It Together Students should meet to finalize the product—a script with a definite beginning and an end that will make sense to viewers.

Step 3: Staging the Hearing

Ask: Does the script succeed in reflecting what happened and give a sense of why McCarthy ultimately failed? (Performers' Perspective)

Directions Student groups will read their script to the entire class. Viewers can take notes and ask questions after the performance.

Putting It Together After the performance, the student groups that wrote the script should meet. They can then decide if they need to revise it in any way based on audience feedback.

Step 4: Critiquing the Script

Ask: Does the role-play or mock hearing succeed in reflecting what happened and give a sense of why McCarthy ultimately failed? (Viewers' Perspective)

Directions Viewers of the performance should divide into groups or meet as a whole to critique the script. Using their notes, viewers should evaluate the script by answering and discussing the following questions:

Hands-On History Chapter Project *Cont.*

The Cold War Begins, 1945–1960

- What was the main message of the script?

- How did the script compare with the description of McCarthyism in the textbook?

- Why did McCarthy's early targets not challenge him when they stood accused?

- Why did support for McCarthy eventually fade?

Putting It Together After the discussion, have students divide into groups and each choose one of the questions above. Give groups a few minutes to agree on an answer. Then have each group recite their answers.

Step 5: Wrap-Up

Ask: What was the impact of McCarthyism? How did it shape American history?

Directions Students should draw from each step of the chapter project to write a brief essay that answers the essential question (above). You may want to give students the option of recording their answer to the essential question and submitting it to you as an audio file.

Putting It Together Students will synthesize the information presented and the discussions following each step to summarize the big idea—how McCarthyism impacted the history of the United States.

Assessing Tell students that their presentation will be assessed based on these factors:

S: Student participates fully and actively in each group of which he or she is a member. Student contributes to all discussions and decision-making in both the smaller group and in the group as a whole. In all activities and research, student exhibits an excellent understanding of how to research and develop the multimedia presentation, of the steps needed in acquiring information and in how to build and present the presentation. Students demonstrate an understanding of how to best display the information and the content of the information does not show grammar flaws or sloppy, incomplete work.

T: Student participates in both the smaller group and the larger class. The student participates in the research and development of the presentation. Students show some understanding of the creation and the content in the presentation.

U: Student participates very little in the group and does little research. The student also has limited input into the research and development of the multimedia presentation that is created.

V: Student rarely participates in any groups, does incomplete and unsatisfactory research and development work, and offers little in the way of input to the rest of the group's needs. Student contributes little or nothing to the research and development of the presentation.

W: The student's work is unacceptable, with little or no participation in any aspect of the activity.

X: The student's work is poor, with no contributions to the group effort.

Technology Extension: Back Channel Discussion during the McCarthyism Script Performance

A back channel discussion is a discussion that takes place while another event, lecture, presentation or performance is taking place. Back channel discussions take place in online chat rooms, through social media sites, or on shared online collaborative documents. Back channel discussions are a fantastic way to elicit student feedback while an event is taking place and it creates an environment where all audience members or students have an equal voice to participate in the discussion. Students who have the opportunity to participate in this type of online discussion will learn how to engage others in a synchronous online discussion, respond to questions thoroughly and compose questions for the class. Back channel discussions allow for all students to participate because they are able to ask questions in an environment that provides extra time and an uninterrupted voice to students who may be typically overshadowed in a class discussion. Students who are typically reluctant to participate in face to face classroom discussions, often find a voice in a back channel discussion that allows them to participate to a great extent. In this EdTechTeacher Technology Extension, you will learn how to create, manage and use a back channel discussion while student groups are performing their McCarthyism scripts.

Creating Back Channel Discussions

There are many Web sites available to educators that can be used to create back channel discussions. These options range from basic chatrooms to private social networks. To learn more about using back channel discussions in the classroom, visit the Using Chatting and Instant Messaging in the Classroom page at EdTechTeacher's Teaching History with Technology site: http://thwt.org/discussion-collaboration/chats/. On this page you will find resources for creating, moderating, and assessing participation in classroom back channel discussions. Tutorials are provided as well as a sample class chat assignment.

Creating McCarthyism Script Back Channel Discussions

Follow the Hands-On Chapter Project as it is described and supplement the project during Step 3 and 4 when student groups perform their scripts and the scripts are critiqued by the class.

Before students complete their scripts for the classroom performance, you will need to either reserve time in a computer lab or use a set of laptops with a wireless Internet connection. While students are performing their McCarthyism script, the rest of the students need to have access to their own computer with Internet access.

During the script performance, the rest of the class should be logged into the classroom chat room, social network or collaborative online document to discuss the performance. You may want to provide specific guidelines for students as they participate in the back channel discussion.

- Does the role-play or mock hearing succeed in reflecting what happened and give a sense of why McCarthy ultimately failed?

- What was the main message of the script?

- How did the script compare with the description of McCarthyism in the textbook?

- Why did McCarthy's early targets not challenge him when they stood accused?

- Why did support for McCarthy eventually fade?

After each group's script performance, you can project the back channel discussion with an LCD projector and have them address any comments, questions or ideas that were mentioned in the back channel during the discussion. You may also have each group review the back channel discussion that was generated during their performance for homework. Upon reviewing the back channel discussion, the group can be responsible for responding to any questions, ideas or comments made during the script performance.

Make clear to students that you will be monitoring and evaluating these transcripts during and after the performance, so all comments should be respectful, even if they are constructively critical.

Assessment and Rubrics

To create rubric to assess the script and back channel discussion, visit the Rubric page at EdTechTeacher's Teaching History with Technology site: http://www.thwt.org/rubrics.html

Additional Online Resources

For additional resources, visit the Cold War page on the Best of History Websites:
http://besthistorysites.net/modern-history/cold-war/

Hands-On History Chapter Project

Postwar America, 1945–1960

A New Peacetime America

ESSENTIAL QUESTION
- *How does prosperity change the way people live?*

Step 1: Facing the Future Students will focus on the amazing changes that took place in U.S. government and culture following World War II, with their final product being a classroom display of items representing these changes.

Directions Have students review Lesson 1, noting the new government programs presented by Presidents Truman and Eisenhower such as the system of interstate highways and the raising of the minimum wage. Have students meet in small groups to research and discuss these changes and how lasting the impact of each has been.

Drawing Conclusions Have students regroup as a class and record what they have found in their research and discussions on the board. After comparing these government programs, then and now, have them draw some conclusions about the effectiveness of the government and the impact it has on their daily lives.

Step 2: New Technologies Americans' buying power increased during this boom time following the war.

Directions Have students read Lesson 2 and remind them that many Americans had new-found wealth in the 1950s and 1960s. What did they spend their money on? Have students note all of the new inventions created and discoveries made in the postwar United States and research others not mentioned in their text.

Putting It Together During their research have them collect photos or drawings of the new developments to be displayed on poster board in their final class presentation.

Step 3: Create a Brochure The United States was bursting with new gadgets after the war years.

Directions Organize students into groups. Have each group select one of the new inventions that appeared in this time period, whether a home device or one used in business or manufacturing. Their task is to create a brochure to sell that product to whomever their buying audience might be—homemakers, businessmen, or choir children, for example. They should write and illustrate their brochures in whatever design they choose. Have the groups present their brochures to the rest of the class, explaining their selling approach and purpose.

Representing Information Give students time to prepare for their presentations. They may role-play or use media other than their posters to present the information. Encourage students to state the topic clearly, describe it, and summarize the information.

Hands-On History Chapter Project *Cont.*

Postwar America, 1945–1960

Step 4: Wrap-Up This activity will synthesize the information that students have collected about the society and culture of this time period.

Directions Divide the class into six teams. Each team should select one presenter to take on the role of an individual who lived during this time period. To avoid duplication among the teams, have each team announce which role their presenter will play. If there are duplicates, assign another role to one of the teams.

Analyzing Information Team members will collaboratively write a journal page from the perspective of the presenter. Each journal page should describe vividly the person's life at this time. Presenters will read the group's journal page to the class. The rest of the class may want to ask the presenters questions. To make the presentations more lively and memorable, presenters may wish to carry relevant signs, dress in costumes, or hold up photos.

Assessing Tell students that their presentation will be assessed based on these factors:

S: Student participates fully and actively in each group of which he or she is a member. Student contributes to all discussions and decision-making in both the smaller group and in the group as a whole. In all activities and research, student exhibits an excellent understanding of how to research and develop the multimedia presentation, of the steps needed in acquiring information and in how to build and present the presentation. Students demonstrate an understanding of how to best display the information and the content of the information does not show grammar flaws or sloppy, incomplete work.

T: Student participates in both the smaller group and the larger class. The student participates in the research and development of the presentation. Students show some understanding of the creation and the content in the presentation.

U: Student participates very little in the group and does little research. The student also has limited input into the research and development of the multimedia presentation that is created.

V: Student rarely participates in any groups, does incomplete and unsatisfactory research and development work, and offers little in the way of input to the rest of the group's needs. Student contributes little or nothing to the research and development of the presentation.

W: The student's work is unacceptable, with little or no participation in any aspect of the activity.

X: The student's work is poor, with no contributions to the group effort.

Technology Extension: New Peacetime America Product Presentation

The end of World War II made America a global superpower, and since the American mainland and its industrial centers were untouched during the war, America became an economic superpower as well. By allowing students to create online poster presentations highlighting a popular invention or "gadget" from the postwar era, the teacher can introduce them to a way to easily create and highlight visual and audio resources as well as text.

Online posters can help provide an audience for student projects well beyond the classroom. They build visual literacy skills, such as how to effectively and persuasively communicate a message. Online posters also challenge critical thinking skills as students have to choose elements to be included or excluded in a poster, as well as how those elements should be integrated and arranged.

Creating Online Posters

To learn more about online posters, visit the Online Posters page at EdTechTeacher's Teaching History with Technology site: http://thwt.org/posters.html. On this page, you can find extensive background information on online posters, tips, links, and other sample activities.

There are several platforms and applications that can be used to create online posters. Online posters not only can include text elements, but also audio and video files. Online posters can be held as "private" (viewable to the invited classroom community only), or "public" (available to the world).

Creating New Peacetime America Product Presentation

Students will proceed with steps 1-3 of the end of the Hands-On Chapter Project as outlined in the project overview, but should be informed that their presentations will take the form of online posters rather than the brochures mentioned. You may want to modify the group task list of the project plan worksheet to include researching and placing sound and video files, as well as text files, on the online poster.

The teacher should follow these steps in completing the lesson:

- **Step 1:** Divide the class into groups. Students should review Lesson 1, particularly noting new government programs proposed by the Truman and Eisenhower Administrations. The groups should conduct online research to find further information about these programs. After sufficient time to research, groups should meet as a class to brainstorm ideas regarding these changes and their impact.

- **Step 2:** Students should read lesson 2. Remind the class that the postwar years were ones of economic boom times and many Americans had newfound wealth in the 1950s and 1960s. Groups should discuss items on which these Americans would have spent that wealth. Students should note inventions and discoveries made in the postwar United States, including those not mentioned in the text. As they continue their online research, they should collect digital copies of photos and drawings of new developments they wish to include in their online posters. If video or audio content exists (for example, archived copies of television commercials for that product), they should include that as well.

- **Step 3:** Once students have had sufficient time to collect information, photos, and drawings of a particular invention or product of the period, they should then create their online poster. Tell students that the purpose of their poster is to create an "ad campaign" to sell the product to their "buying audience" (homemakers, businessmen, children, etc.) When posters are completed, have each group present their results to the class as a whole, explaining their selling approach and purpose.

Once posters are completed, arrange for student groups to demonstrate their online work either in front of the class or by assigning it to be viewed as homework. The teacher may wish to have students write comments or journal entries about each "gadget" explaining why they would (or would not) want to purchase that item.

Assessment and Rubrics

You may want to integrate research, creativity, and layout techniques into the project rubrics. For further information regarding rubric construction, visit http://thwt.org/rubrics.html

Additional Online Resources

For more Web sites, lesson plans, and activities related to the post World War II era, visit the Best of History Websites Cold War Era page: http://besthistorysites.net/american-history/cold-war-era/

Hands-On History Chapter Project

The New Frontier and the Great Society, 1960–1968

What is a Great Society?

ESSENTIAL QUESTION

- *Can government fix society's problems?*

Step 1: How Court Decisions Affect Society Today In the first of four activities relating to what makes a great society, students will use information in the lesson to relate 1960s Supreme Court decisions to modern American life.

Directions Have students review the Court decisions made during the 1960s. Then ask them to research newspaper, library, or Internet sources to find a recent event or legal decision that relates to decisions made by the Supreme Court during the 1960s. Have them explain the connection between the recent event and the original Court decision.

Comparing and Contrasting In their presentations, students will discuss ways in which the current event is similar to or different from an event that led to a 1960s Supreme Court decision.

Step 2: Motivational Speeches Students will research memorable speeches made by leaders, writers, and citizens that relate to the building of a great society.

Directions Have students conduct newspaper, library, or Internet research to find speeches made by people throughout history. Speeches may be historical or current. Students may research speeches made by Americans or other citizens of the world. Encourage students to find a speech that is aimed at the building of an improved or just society. Students should find speeches that are inspirational to them.

Analyzing Primary Sources Students will select the parts of the speech that are most relevant and inspirational to share with the rest of the class, either as oral presentations or in typed papers.

Step 3: Creating a Peace Corps or VISTA Work Plan Students will explore responsibilities of citizenship by taking on the role of a Peace Corps or VISTA volunteer.

Directions Discuss why the VISTA and Peace Corps programs are part of a "great society" in terms of a nation's responsibility to its citizens and to other nations. Have students research the types of projects that VISTA and the Peace Corps tackle. Then have each student choose an area of the United States or of another country in which to "volunteer." Ask each student to create a work plan that includes identification of a problem, a specific goal they hope to accomplish, equipment or resources needed, tasks required to achieve the goal, and a schedule for completing the tasks.

Identifying Problems and Solutions By breaking societal problems into achievable steps, students will learn how to find and implement solutions.

Hands-On History Chapter Project *Cont.*

The New Frontier and the Great Society, 1960–1968

Step 4: Wrap-Up Creating a Great Society Poster Students will discuss what qualities make up a society that can be considered "great" and create a poster illustrating those qualities.

Directions Hang a poster on the wall with the title "A Great Society." Ask the class what societies they have studied—such as ancient Greece—that they consider great. Then ask them to list the qualities that are important in a great society. Use their list as headings for columns on the poster.

Analyzing Information Students will analyze the domestic programs, foreign policies, and court decisions of the 1960s and list below the headings on the poster those items that illustrate each quality.

Assessing Tell students that their presentation will be assessed based on these factors:

S: Student participates fully and actively in each group of which he or she is a member. Student contributes to all discussions and decision-making in both the smaller group and in the group as a whole. In all activities and research, student exhibits an excellent understanding of how to research and develop the multimedia presentation, of the steps needed in acquiring information and in how to build and present the presentation. Students demonstrate an understanding of how to best display the information and the content of the information does not show grammar flaws or sloppy, incomplete work.

T: Student participates in both the smaller group and the larger class. The student participates in the research and development of the presentation. Students show some understanding of the creation and the content in the presentation.

U: Student participates very little in the group and does little research. The student also has limited input into the research and development of the multimedia presentation that is created.

V: Student rarely participates in any groups, does incomplete and unsatisfactory research and development work, and offers little in the way of input to the rest of the group's needs. Student contributes little or nothing to the research and development of the presentation.

W: The student's work is unacceptable, with little or no participation in any aspect of the activity.

X: The student's work is poor, with no contributions to the group effort.

Technology Extension: VoiceThread Motivational Speeches

In this EdTechTeacher Technology Extension, we will help you expand your Hands-On Chapter Project to include a VoiceThread for **Step 2: Motivational Speeches**. VoiceThread is a collaborative platform for adding text, video, and voice comments to uploaded images, videos, and other content. Once your students select and share relevant components of the inspirational speeches, they can record audio commentary or input supporting text. Through an online platform like a blog, wiki, Web site, e-mail or unique VoiceThread URL, there are many opportunities to share the VoiceThreads and incorporate the project into further exercises. You may task students to provide direct feedback on peer projects, have family and friends provide comments, use it for student self-evaluation or introduce them as examples for future classes. Either way, VoiceThread is a dynamic tool that allows you to collaborate asynchronously, reach a wider audience and provide students multiple ways to be creative and show competency.

Creating a VoiceThread

VoiceThread is an online application allowing you to upload images, videos, documents, and presentations, into a central location and then invite others to add comments. These asynchronous conversations take place whenever it is convenient for your audience to access the Internet and participate. VoiceThread allows viewers to comment on the content in five different ways: by voice (using a microphone or telephone), by text, by audio file, or by video. Depending on your desired reach, VoiceThreads can be kept private or you can publish them on the VoiceThread site, email a link or embed them on other platforms such as wikis and blogs.

Your students may create their own accounts with a valid e-mail address or you can create an educator account and provide each student an identity to use for recording comments. If you plan to use VoiceThread in class, then each student should have their own account so multiple comments can be recorded at the same time. There are benefits to each option, which can be explored at the VoiceThread page at EdTechTeacher's Teaching History with Technology site: http://thwt.org/multimedia/voicethread/. On this page you will find examples, tutorials, rubrics, and suggestions on how to integrate them into your classroom.

Creating a VoiceThread focused on a Motivational Speech

In this activity, students will create a VoiceThread highlighting memorable speeches made by leaders, writers, and citizens that relate to the building of a great society. Students can choose from various multimedia options to share their inspirational speech and supplement it with an audio commentary or text.

Once students have signed up for VoiceThread, review a sample that you have created to highlight VoiceThread functionality and familiarize students with the tools. Discuss positive features of your sample as a class and then set expectations for student work referencing your assessment criteria.

Once students have conducted their research and identified an inspirational speech, they should brainstorm ways to present their content and partner with a classmate to discuss. VoiceThread offers students many formats to personalize their presentations and dynamically represent their understanding of building a great society. Students should create a draft of their VoiceThread and consult with their partner for peer feedback on the effort. Using the feedback and project expectations students can now finalize their VoiceThreads for publishing.

Publish the VoiceThreads and require that each student leave comments on at least five other students' products. Tasking them to give feedback on specific features will help students to stay focused and provide you more detailed representations of their understanding. Also, have students complete a self-assessment for their product after having explored classmates' projects. It will be beneficial for students to be able to evaluate the quality of their own work so they can better edit their own content in the future.

Once finished, you may choose to make the VoiceThreads public for family and friends or to keep them private for viewing only within your class.

Assessment and Rubrics

To assess the project and create a rubric for the VoiceThread projects, visit the Rubrics page at EdTechTeacher's Teaching History with Technology site: http://www.thwt.org/rubrics.html.

Additional Online Resources

Creative Commons: Creative Commons is a nonprofit organization that develops, supports, and stewards legal and technical infrastructure that maximizes digital creativity, sharing, and innovation. Help students navigate Internet searches at Teaching History with Technology: http://thwt.org/creativecommons.html

Hands-On History Chapter Project

The Civil Rights Movement, 1954–1968

A Freedom Drama

ESSENTIAL QUESTION

- *Why do you think the civil rights movement made gains in postwar America?*

Step 1: We Shall Overcome Remind students that U.S. history is filled with dramatic events. In Step 1 students will create the first of a theatrical presentation that chronicles the history of freedom for African Americans in the United States.

Directions Discuss the experiences of African Americans under laws that enforced discrimination. Have students give their views on how they would have felt in similar circumstances. Organize students into groups. Assign each group to research a different African American (a farmer, a teacher, a civil-rights activist) prior to the civil rights movement and desegregation. Each group should write a monologue about the experiences of their person. Encourage students to share sensory elements in their monologues. Have the characters let the class know what they saw, heard, smelled, and felt.

Putting It Together Have group members read the monologues aloud. Have the class comment how effectively the monologues help them to understand the experiences of African Americans prior to desegregation.

Step 2: Freedom News Students will continue their theatrical presentation by writing news stories about the Montgomery bus boycott.

Directions Discuss the events related to the Montgomery bus boycott, such as the arrest of Rosa Parks and Martin Luther King's leadership of the movement. Have groups write scripts for a television news report about the bus boycott. Students should feel free to infer the feelings of the people represented in their news story while sticking to the known facts.

Putting It Together Have groups read their news scripts to the class.

Step 3: Securing Voting Rights Students will continue work on their theatrical presentations of the civil rights movement by writing a voting-rights debate scene.

Directions Discuss African-American struggles to gain voting rights and the opposition they faced. Once again, organize students into groups. Ask each group to research viewpoints on either side of the voting rights debate. Have groups use their research to write a debate scene representing viewpoints for and against a voting rights act. Encourage students to incorporate quotes from their research into their debate scenes. Students should also create posters as props for the scene. The posters should use actual slogans from the period.

Putting It Together Have groups present their scenes. Ask students to compare past and present attitudes about the role of African Americans in politics.

Hands-On History Chapter Project *Cont.*

The Civil Rights Movement, 1954–1968

Step 4: Wrap-Up Students will finish the process they started in Step 1.

Directions As a class, review the news reports, debate scenes, and monologues that each group created. Decide if any scenes should be shortened or combined. Make any revisions needed to the writing, including corrections for spelling, mechanics, and word choice. Next, decide on the order in which the scenes will be presented. The teacher should assign roles to student actors. Have the class select a student to act as director to oversee staging the drama.

Putting It Together Finally, have the class present their drama to another class or to the school. Encourage the class and audience to discuss their thoughts and feelings about the civil rights movement and its impact on the growth of freedom and democracy in the United States.

Assessing Tell students that their presentation will be assessed based on these factors:

S: Student participates fully and actively in each group of which he or she is a member. Student contributes to all discussions and decision-making in both the smaller group and in the group as a whole. In all activities and research, student exhibits an excellent understanding of how to research and develop the multimedia presentation, of the steps needed in acquiring information and in how to build and present the presentation. Students demonstrate an understanding of how to best display the information and the content of the information does not show grammar flaws or sloppy, incomplete work.

T: Student participates in both the smaller group and the larger class. The student participates in the research and development of the presentation. Students show some understanding of the creation and the content in the presentation.

U: Student participates very little in the group and does little research. The student also has limited input into the research and development of the multimedia presentation that is created.

V: Student rarely participates in any groups, does incomplete and unsatisfactory research and development work, and offers little in the way of input to the rest of the group's needs. Student contributes little or nothing to the research and development of the presentation.

W: The student's work is unacceptable, with little or no participation in any aspect of the activity.

X: The student's work is poor, with no contributions to the group effort.

Technology Extension: Video and Analysis

Your students will already be writing and performing three preliminary theatrical presentations based on the history of freedom for African Americans in the United States, so let's also create a lasting record of those performances. In this EdTechTeacher Technology Extension, we will provide an overview to help you facilitate the filming of your class performances, make them accessible online, and design a process for analysis and feedback. The inclusion of student videos in your project will help increase student motivation and allow for a more detailed analysis of the content and performances prior to the final live presentation. Once the performances have been made viewable through an online platform like a blog or Web site, there are many opportunities to further incorporate the footage into exercises. You may choose to have family and friends provide comments, ask students to direct feedback on specific peer presentation elements, use it for student self-evaluation or introduce them as examples for future classes. Either way, the recording of in-class performances extends the learning beyond the in-class activity and deepens the experience.

Filming and Publishing Videos

Depending on your resources and goals, you can create professional level videos with green screen technology or simply use your Web cam, smartphone, or digital camera. It is very important that your performances are audible, so practice with your recording device beforehand to ensure it can capture the level of audio and visual quality you desire. Furthermore, editing tools are available to hone the project or you can have the product be left as a one-take production. Once your video is completed, you may choose to upload the performance to a Web site or blog for viewing. Organizing all of the presentations into an easy-to-view format will be an important component of the exercise. To learn more about creating and setting up this type of project, visit the Video page at EdTechTeacher's Teaching History with Technology site: http://thwt.org/video.html. On this page you'll find a brief overview of using video in the classroom and examples of video projects.

Creating Videos of your Class Performances

By following the Hands-On Chapter Project, your students will be well-prepared to act out the three written and designed performances. The key features in a successful video extension will be testing your recording device to be sure it produces a quality recording, identifying a location to place the camera for each performance, determining how you will make the videos accessible to viewers and planning how to use the videos afterwards.

Dramatic Performances

Communicate to students that they will be working in groups to write, design, and act in multiple performances that will help address the essential question: **Why do you think the civil rights movement made gains in postwar America?** Set expectations for students with regard to length, vocabulary, content, props, costumes, and time lines. Utilizing all of the comments and discussions from the first three performances, have a whole class discussion that serves to prepare them for the final live presentation. Follow the Hands-On Chapter Project Step 4 to complete the activity.

Video Sharing

Numerous video sharing sites exist that make it easy to have a whole class post their videos in one place. While some of the most popular, such as YouTube, are blocked at many schools, most schools do not filter educational video sharing sites, such as those listed at http://thwt.org/video.html. For nearly all video sharing sites, you can create a private channel so only those whom you invite can view your videos, or you can post your videos on a public channel. Just be sure that students do not disclose personal information. Posting videos to a blog, wiki, or Web site will allow for easy commenting from peers, which is something that is very important when choosing how you will publish the performances.

Video Analysis

Using the videos will allow classmates to review the performances multiple times and assess how the essential question has been addressed. Once the videos have been made public, students should answer specific questions, which you have highlighted. If you post the videos on a video sharing site, then students can answer these questions as comments posted below the videos. You can have an entire, asynchronous "class discussion" that takes place online. To help hold students accountable for closely watching each other's videos, review their comments in class and have them explain why they responded in a particular way. If you are unable to publish to a site that allows viewers to leave feedback; have students type their responses and submit them via e-mail, a drop box, or as a printout.

Assessment and Rubrics

To assess your student performance in the presentations, you will want to identify key categories, such as contribution, persuasive content, and props. You may also focus on the students' ability to critically analyze the videos and respond with constructive comments. For more information about creating rubrics for video analysis, visit http://thwt.org/rubrics.html.

Additional Online Resources

For more Web sites, lesson plans, and activities related to civil rights movement, visit the Best of History Sites Page: http://besthistorysites.net/american-history/civil-rights/

Hands-On History Chapter Project

The Vietnam War, 1954–1975

Create a Documentary of the Vietnam War

ESSENTIAL QUESTION
- *How does military conflict divide people within cultures?*

Step 1: Determining the Theme

Directions Write the essential question on the board and explain to students that in this first step, different groups will create the basic storyline for a documentary of the Vietnam War. For example, a documentary could describe the battles of the war, the U.S. presidents conducting the war, army life, or life at home during the war.

Putting It Together Later, each group should make a presentation to persuade the others about the merits of their choice. (Students could think about the arguments and style a young filmmaker might use to persuade potential backers about backing his or her project.)

Step 2: Planning the Video

Ask: What were the key developments in the chosen story, and what were the historical results?

Directions Students should use their textbook and other research to outline the basic issue and the chronology. A second team could concentrate on thinking visually. This team would have to collaborate closely with the first and research photos in magazines and newspapers or video clips of the period.

Putting It Together When the teams meet, they can decide on the "storyboards" for the video—sketches representing each shot in the 10 scenes (or whatever number seems appropriate) so that the topic is covered from beginning to end.

Step 3: Creating the Script or Voice-over

Ask: What is the core of the message, and how can it be conveyed with images?

Directions Students may need to re-assess their storyboards and edit them as they go through them to write the script or "voice-over" for the video or as they create the visuals. The writing will need to be concise and focus on the essential point of what is happening in each scene. Students can divide up in teams to write the voice-over for two or more storyboards.

Putting It Together The teams can meet to review and edit their final script.

Hands-On History Chapter Project *Cont.*

The Vietnam War, 1954–1975

Step 4: Presenting the Documentaries

Ask: What is the message of the documentary?

Directions Allow class time to view the completed documentaries. After each showing, engage the class by asking them to answer the following questions during a class discussion:

- What was the message of the documentary?

- How was the message conveyed? Was it clear?

- What information was "left out" of the documentary?

- What were the best parts of the documentary? Why?

- How could the documentary be improved?

Putting It Together The class should determine as a whole if the documentaries reflected information from the textbook, and if the information was portrayed accurately.

Assessing Tell students that their presentation will be assessed based on these factors:

S: Student participates fully and actively in each group of which he or she is a member. Student contributes to all discussions and decision-making in both the smaller group and in the group as a whole. In all activities and research, student exhibits an excellent understanding of how to research and develop the multimedia presentation, of the steps needed in acquiring information and in how to build and present the presentation. Students demonstrate an understanding of how to best display the information and the content of the information does not show grammar flaws or sloppy, incomplete work.

T: Student participates in both the smaller group and the larger class. The student participates in the research and development of the presentation. Students show some understanding of the creation and the content in the presentation.

U: Student participates very little in the group and does little research. The student also has limited input into the research and development of the multimedia presentation that is created.

V: Student rarely participates in any groups, does incomplete and unsatisfactory research and development work, and offers little in the way of input to the rest of the group's needs. Student contributes little or nothing to the research and development of the presentation.

W: The student's work is unacceptable, with little or no participation in any aspect of the activity.

X: The student's work is poor, with no contributions to the group effort.

21st Century Learning

Technology Extension: Vietnam War Documentary Comic Activity

By allowing students to create online comics, they are forced to demonstrate their understanding of content and gain a greater appreciation of historical concepts and ideas. While comics were long derided as distractions for children, the emergence of graphic novels as a serious form of art and literature has made educators take a second look at the possibilities of communicating through art and words. Comic creation is an easy way to create and share ideas and philosophies of various groups and individuals who were "major players" during the Vietnam War era.

Creating comics develops analytical and critical thinking skills. Opportunities exist for students to include "speech bubbles" or "text bubbles," thereby demonstrating knowledge of concepts and facts of the period.

Creating Comics

To learn more about comic creation, visit the Comics page at EdTechTeacher's Teaching History with Technology Comics page: http://thwt.org/comics.html. Here, you will find a large variety of tools, links, and sample lessons dealing with comic creation. Lesson plans and ideas, as well as sample comics and rubrics are also available.

Several free or inexpensive comic creation applications are available for teachers and students. Many are "drag and drop" in nature, and some also allow the user to create or import their own art. Many comic creator sites also allow the user to embed the comic into a Web page or share online.

Creating Vietnam War Documentary Comics

Students will proceed with steps 1–3 of the end of Hands-On Chapter Project as outlined in the project overview. Be sure to make the class aware that they will be creating comic books with computer technology rather than developing traditional storyboards for a documentary. As stated in the overview, the class should be broken up into groups and tasks should be assigned in order to create an acceptable finished product.

Student groups can conduct historical research, collaborate to consider the "visual" aspect of the project, and write a suitable script for the comic documentary. The group should show significant planning in development of the comic.

Recommended steps to complete this project include:

Step 1: The teacher should write the "essential question" on the board or overhead. The question is **"How does military conflict divide people within cultures?"** Explain to students that they will be working in "teams" to create a comic "documentary" of the Vietnam War era. After dividing the class into teams, groups should decide the basic "storyline" for the comic. For example, will the group focus on the battles of the war, the role of U.S. presidents during the war, the life of soldiers during the conflict, or the "war at home."

Step 2: Students should begin planning their comic by looking for information that helps answer the question: "What were the key developments in the group's chosen story, and what were the historical results?" After reading the question, have students conduct online research as well as traditional methods of research, including using the textbook, to outline basic issues and chronology that will be featured in the comic. You should also encourage the group to develop ideas by "thinking visually," by looking at videos as well as newspaper and magazine stories from the period. Have groups develop "storyboards" or visual frames that will make up the basic framework of their comic.

Step 3: Read the question: "What is the core of the message, and how can it be conveyed with images?" In this phase, students should continue to review and refine their storyboards as well as edit those storyboards as they develop a "script" for their comic. Students can divide into sub-teams in order to write scripts or dialog for various numbers of storyboards.

Step 4: You should announce the final question: "What is the message of the documentary?" Once groups have completed their comics, allow for time for the entire class to view each of the completed comics. After each viewing, engage the class by asking them to answer the following questions in class discussion:

- What was the message of the comic?

- How was the message conveyed? Was it clear?

- What information was "left out" of the comic?

- What were the best parts of the comic? Why?

- How could the comic be improved?

As a group, the class should also determine whether the comics reflected information from the textbook and if the information was portrayed accurately.

Assessment and Rubrics

Advice about creating rubrics for comics can be found on the EdTechTeacher's Teaching History with Technology Comics page: http://thwt.org/comics.html. In addition, further information on rubrics can be found at the EdTechTeacher's Teaching History with Technology rubrics page, located at http://thwt.org/rubrics.html.

Additional Online Resources

Further Resources: For more Web sites, lesson plans, and activities related to the Vietnam War era, visit the Best of History Websites Vietnam page: http://besthistorysites.net/american-history/vietnam/.

Hands-On History Chapter Project

The Politics of Protest, 1960–1980

Presenting a Historical Drama

ESSENTIAL QUESTION

- *How has society changed for students, women, LGBTQ activists, and Latinos?*

Step 1: Assigning Groups Small groups of students receive their assignments

Directions Organize the class into groups and have each prepare a dramatic presentation on one of the situations below or another of their choice. Encourage all students to participate, and have each group present their skit to the rest of the class.

- a brother and sister in college trying to explain the counterculture to their parents

- a group of women at the first meeting of the National Organization for Women, setting goals and planning action

- a group of Latino farm workers discussing the benefits and risks of a strike

Putting It Together Encourage students to begin a separate section of their notebooks to take notes on the chapter from the perspective of the Americans they will role-play.

Step 2: Write and Plan the Drama Students begin to write their scripts, including lines and stage directions. They create any props they might need, such as posters, signs, buttons, or headbands.

Directions Remind students that their dramas should be based on the content of the lesson. Written scripts can be rough guides, with students free to improvise. Props should be appropriate to protests of the time and the situation they will enact.

Putting It Together Ask students to read each other's drafts and suggest changes for the second draft.

Step 3: Present the Drama Students rehearse and present their dramas. They watch the dramas of other groups.

Directions Remind students that scripts can be rough guides. They are free to improvise during the dramatization, as long as any ad-libbed lines are based on the content of the lesson. Have students rehearse until they are comfortable and ready to present. Students should be attentive during the presentations of other groups.

Putting It Together As students do their presentations, ask the class to take notes as to the historical accuracy of the presentation.

Step 4: Wrap-Up

Directions Ask groups to write a review of the dramas presented by the other two groups. Have groups share the reviews with each other.

Hands-On History Chapter Project *Cont.*

The Politics of Protest, 1960–1980

Putting It Together After groups have read the reviews, ask them to make any corrections for accuracy and present the dramas to the class again.

Assessing Tell students that their presentation will be assessed based on these factors:

S: Student participates fully and actively in each group of which he or she is a member. Student contributes to all discussions and decision-making in both the smaller group and in the group as a whole. In all activities and research, student exhibits an excellent understanding of how to research and develop the multimedia presentation, of the steps needed in acquiring information and in how to build and present the presentation. Students demonstrate an understanding of how to best display the information and the content of the information does not show grammar flaws or sloppy, incomplete work.

T: Student participates in both the smaller group and the larger class. The student participates in the research and development of the presentation. Students show some understanding of the creation and the content in the presentation.

U: Student participates very little in the group and does little research. The student also has limited input into the research and development of the multimedia presentation that is created.

V: Student rarely participates in any groups, does incomplete and unsatisfactory research and development work, and offers little in the way of input to the rest of the group's needs. Student contributes little or nothing to the research and development of the presentation.

W: The student's work is unacceptable, with little or no participation in any aspect of the activity.

X: The student's work is poor, with no contributions to the group effort.

Technology Extension: Videotaping a Dramatic Presentation

In this EdTechTeacher Technology Extension, we will provide an overview to help you facilitate the filming of your class performances, make them accessible online, and design a process for publishing student reviews. Your students will already be writing and performing a skit based on how society has changed for students, women, LGBTQ activists, and Latinos. This Technology extension activity provides an opportunity to create a lasting record of this work. The inclusion of student videos in your project will help increase student motivation and allow for a more detailed analysis of the content and performance. Once the skits have been made viewable through an online platform like a blog, wiki, Web site or e-mail, there are many opportunities to further incorporate the footage into exercises. You may choose to have family and friends provide comments, ask students to direct feedback on peer presentation elements, use it for student self-evaluation or introduce them as examples for future classes. Either way, the recording of in-class performances extends the learning beyond the live presentation.

Filming and Publishing Videos

Depending on your resources and goals, you can create professional-level videos with green screen technology or simply use your Web cam, smart phone, or digital camera. It is very important that your performances are audible so practice with your recording device beforehand to ensure it can capture the level of audio and visual quality you desire. Furthermore, editing tools are available to hone the project, or you can have the product be left as a one-take production. Once your video is completed, it can be uploaded to Web sites, blogs, or third-party sites where you can get a link for distribution. To learn more about creating and setting up this type of project, visit the Video page at EdTechTeacher's Teaching History with Technology site: http://thwt.org/video.html. On this page you'll find a brief overview of using video in the classroom and examples of video projects.

Creating Videos of Your Class Performances

By following the Hands-On Chapter Project, your students will be well-prepared to act out their own written and designed dramas. The key elements in a successful video extension will be testing your recording device to be sure it produces a quality recording, identifying a location to place the camera for the performance, determining how you will make the video accessible to viewers, and planning how to use the video afterward.

Dramatic Performance

Communicate to students that they will be working in groups to write, design, and act in a filmed skit that will portray how society has changed for students, women, LGBTQ activists, and Latinos in the United States. Set expectations for students with regard to script length, vocabulary, content, props, costumes, and other aspects of the final skit.

Allow students to choose from the three suggested plots or advise them to design their own (with your approval). Using time in class, groups will write their scripts based on what they have learned from the textbook and from previous lessons. To support the scripts, students will want to identify stage directions, props, and costumes that will help their performances come to life.

Once groups have completed a draft of their performance they should partner with another group and do a read-through. This will provide a round of peer feedback and help students gain confidence in their assigned roles. Groups should edit their scripts based on received feedback and continue to rehearse. Some groups may choose to ad lib lines, but it is important that each member feels comfortable with this style of performance as it may increase anxiety.

Students should perform their dramas for the class.

Video Sharing

Numerous video sharing sites exist that make it easy to have a whole class post their videos in one place. While some of the most popular, such as YouTube, are blocked at many schools, most schools do not filter educational video sharing sites, such as those listed at http://thwt.org/video.html. For nearly all video sharing sites, you can create a private channel so only those whom you invite can view your videos, or you can post your videos on a public channel. Just be sure that students do not disclose personal information. Posting videos to a blog, wiki or Web site will allow for easy commenting from peers which is something that should be considered when choosing how you will publish the performances.

Video Analysis

The videos will provide classmates an opportunity to review the skits multiple times and assess how the essential question has been answered. Once the videos have been made public, students should answer the questions listed below. If you choose to publish to a site that allows viewers to leave feedback, have the students post after each commercial. Otherwise, have students type their responses and submit them via electronic mail, a drop box, or as a printout.

- Review two of your classmates' skits and take notes.

- Comment in your own words on the following;

  - What was the context of the skit?

  - Who were the characters in the skit?

  - What was the most compelling component of the skit? Why?

  - What changes would you make to the skit? Why?

  - Name one similarity and one difference between your skit and your classmates'.

- Review your own drama and comment on your group's performance. After viewing your classmates' skits what changes would you make to your own?

Assessment and Rubrics

To assess your student performance in the presentations, you will want to identify key categories. For more information about creating rubrics for video analysis, visit http://thwt.org/rubrics.html.

Additional Online Resources

For more Web sites, lesson plans, and activities related to the American society in the 1960s and 1970s, visit the Best of History Websites Cold War Era page: http://besthistorysites.net/american-history/cold-war-era/

Hands-On History Chapter Project

Politics and Economics, 1968–1980

Oral History of the 1970s

ESSENTIAL QUESTION
- *How does society change the shape of itself over time?*

Step 1: Researching the Topic Divide the class into small groups. Ask groups to choose one of the following topics: the civil rights movement, the environmental movement, or the Watergate scandal.

Putting It Together Have students use library and Internet sources to find photographs that show a dramatic moment relevant to their topic. (For example, Nixon flashing the "victory" sign after he resigned, or photos of the first Earth Day.) Have students print out the photographs and save them for use later in the project.

Step 2: Preparing for the Interview Tell students that each of them will be conducting an interview with someone who was a teenager or an adult in the 1970s.

Putting It Together Have students in groups prepare a list of questions they want to ask interview subjects about their topic. Questions should center on the interviewee's recollections of the events related to the chosen topic. Each student will be conducting their own interview, but have students discuss amongst themselves who would be the most interesting interviewees. Whenever possible, encourage students to choose interviewees of different backgrounds and ages.

Step 3: Conducting the Interview Students should arrange the interview and be prepared to take notes. (Or, students may ask permission to record the interview.) In addition, students should show interviewees the photographs they selected and ask interviewees to comment on them.

Putting It Together After the interview, students should meet back in their groups to discuss and compare what they have learned from the interviews.

Step 4: Summarizing the Information Have students in groups collaboratively write an essay about their topic. Encourage students to draw upon information from the chapter as well as their interviews.

Putting It Together In their essays, students should clearly delineate between the events that surrounded their topic and the reaction of people to those events at the time.

Step 5: Presenting the Project Visually Students should try to integrate the information presented in this chapter, their research, and their notes based on the interviews.

Putting It Together Have students create and illustrate a poster presenting an overview of their topic using the photographs and excerpts from their interviews.

Hands-On History Chapter Project *Cont.*

Politics and Economics, 1968–1980

Step 6: Wrap-Up Students should present their final project to the class. They should explain what they learned in their research and interviews. Display final projects in the classroom.

Putting It Together Ask students to evaluate their completed projects by answering the following questions in writing:

- Which part of the project was most demanding? Why?

- Which part of the project was the most interesting to me? Why?

- What did I learn from this project about American history?

Assessing Tell students that their presentation will be assessed based on these factors:

S: Student participates fully and actively in each group of which he or she is a member. Student contributes to all discussions and decision-making in both the smaller group and in the group as a whole. In all activities and research, student exhibits an excellent understanding of how to research and develop the multimedia presentation, of the steps needed in acquiring information and in how to build and present the presentation. Students demonstrate an understanding of how to best display the information and the content of the information does not show grammar flaws or sloppy, incomplete work.

T: Student participates in both the smaller group and the larger class. The student participates in the research and development of the presentation. Students show some understanding of the creation and the content in the presentation.

U: Student participates very little in the group and does little research. The student also has limited input into the research and development of the multimedia presentation that is created.

V: Student rarely participates in any groups, does incomplete and unsatisfactory research and development work, and offers little in the way of input to the rest of the group's needs. Student contributes little or nothing to the research and development of the presentation.

W: The student's work is unacceptable, with little or no participation in any aspect of the activity.

X: The student's work is poor, with no contributions to the group effort.

21st Century Learning

Technology Extension: Oral History of the 1970s Podcast Project

Oral history projects take on a new dynamic by giving students an opportunity to create podcasts of their interviews. Through podcasting, students can more easily create and share multimedia projects as well as develop interviewing and historical research skills. Podcasts can also be stored and retrieved for future use, and easily played on computers, smartphones, or portable media players.

Podcasts are digital audio and/or video files that can be downloaded or made available via RSS ("really simple syndication") subscription. This EdTechTeacher Technology Extension will help the teacher develop skills and strategies to effectively create podcasts.

Creating Podcasts

To learn more about podcasting, access the Podcasts page at the EdTechTeacher's Teaching History with Technology page: http://thwt.org/historypodcasts.html. Background information on podcasting, as well as tips, links, and other sample activities is available, including video tutorials for common podcasting tools and platforms. RSS feeds are also explained.

Several applications are available to create podcasts, and many computer platforms include podcast-creation software. Projects can be kept very simple by only allowing students to record audio in one take, or they can be made more sophisticated by allowing students to use editing tools. Finally, podcasts can be hosted on a school server, a Web-based podcast host, or an external server site.

Creating an Oral History of the 1970s Podcast

Students should proceed through steps 1–6 of the end of the Hands-On Chapter Project, but should utilize podcast technology rather than a traditional oral history interview. Since each student will be conducting a separate podcast interview, it is advisable to select interviewees of varied ages and backgrounds. Students should also adequately prepare for the podcast interview by writing questions prior to the interview, as well acquiring permission from interview subjects prior to beginning the podcast procedure.

To complete the project, the teacher should follow the steps outlined below:

Step 1: Divide the class into small groups. Each group should select one of these topics as it relates to the 1970s:

- The civil rights movement in the 1970s

- The 1970s environmental movement

- Watergate

Once student groups are created, they should use traditional and Internet sources to develop concepts and find information about their assigned topic. Encourage the groups to look for visual sources that highlight their topic, such as Nixon's famous "victory sign" wave after he resigned from office, or photos of the first Earth Day. If students create video podcasts (sometimes called vodcasts), they can copy or scan photos to use in their podcast.

Step 2: Once students have completed their research, have them formulate a set of questions they want to ask interview subjects about the topic. Questions should center on the interviewee's recollections of the events related to the chosen topic. Each student will be conducting their own interview and creating their own podcast, but have students discuss amongst themselves who would be the most interesting interviewees. Encourage students to choose interviewees of different ages and backgrounds. However, interviewees should be old enough to have reasonable recollections of the events of the 1970s.

Step 3: Next, students should conduct the interview and create the podcast. Podcasts should be conducted in a location with a minimum of background noise. Once recordings are completed, students can finish editing, conversion, and storage procedures for podcasts.

Step 4: Once podcasts have been completed, students can collaboratively listen to podcasted material and compare and contrast what was mentioned by different interview subjects. The teacher may wish to have student groups write essays showing the comparison and contrast. If so, make arrangements to have computers available (with word processing software), or allot sufficient time to use the school computer lab.

Step 5: Students should present their podcasts in class in front of all students. The class can discuss how interviewees' recollections compare with material in the chapter.

Step 6: After presenting their completed podcasts, ask students to reflect on the project by writing an essay answering the following questions:

- Which part of the project was most demanding? Why?

- Which part of the project was the most interesting to me? Why?

- What did I learn from this project about American history?

Assessment and Rubrics

The teacher will want to integrate assessment categories such as sound effects, transitions, interview techniques, and creativity in the rubric. For further information regarding rubric construction, visit http://thwt.org/rubrics.html.

Additional Online Resources

For more Web sites, lesson plans, and activities related to the 1970s, visit the Best of History Web sites Cold War Era page: http://besthistorysites.net/american-history/cold-war-era/.

Hands-On History Chapter Project

The Resurgence of Conservatism, 1980–1992

Conducting an Opinion Poll

ESSENTIAL QUESTION
- *How do you think the resurgence of conservative ideas has changed society?*

Step 1: Listing Priorities Tell students they will be conducting an opinion poll on President Ronald Reagan's performance as president.

Directions Have small groups of students review the material presented in Lesson 1 to compile a list of the issues that were most important to Americans in the 1980s.

Step 2: Preparing the Poll Keeping in mind the list of issues they compiled in Step 1, students should review the material presented in Lesson 2.

Directions Ask student groups to choose five issues and compose a statement for each issue that assesses President Reagan's job performance.

Step 3: Conducting the Poll Each student should arrange to interview at least one person who was of voting age in the 1980s. The student should then read each of the statements composed during Step 2 and ask the respondent if he or she agrees or disagrees with the statement.

Directions Respondents should be given five options, ranked by number: (1) strongly disagree; (2) disagree; (3) neutral; (4) agree; or (5) strongly agree. Encourage students to ask follow-up questions if respondents express a strong opinion on an issue.

Step 4: Analyzing the Findings Have students return to their groups and compare their poll results.

Directions Ask students to calculate the average response to each of their statements, and then write a brief paragraph for each in which they attempt to interpret their findings.

Step 5: Wrap Up Have groups share their results with the rest of the class. Encourage students to discuss why President Reagan scored higher on some students' polls than others.

Putting It Together Have students evaluate the project by answering the following questions:

- What was the most difficult part of the project? Why?

- What was the best part of the project? Why?

- What was the most important thing I learned by completing this project?

Ask students to record their responses in their journal.

Hands-On History Chapter Project *Cont.*

The Resurgence of Conservatism, 1980–1992

Assessing Tell students that their presentation will be assessed based on these factors:

S: Student participates fully and actively in each group of which he or she is a member. Student contributes to all discussions and decision-making in both the smaller group and in the group as a whole. In all activities and research, student exhibits an excellent understanding of how to research and develop the multimedia presentation, of the steps needed in acquiring information and in how to build and present the presentation. Students demonstrate an understanding of how to best display the information and the content of the information does not show grammar flaws or sloppy, incomplete work.

T: Student participates in both the smaller group and the larger class. The student participates in the research and development of the presentation. Students show some understanding of the creation and the content in the presentation.

U: Student participates very little in the group and does little research. The student also has limited input into the research and development of the multimedia presentation that is created.

V: Student rarely participates in any groups, does incomplete and unsatisfactory research and development work, and offers little in the way of input to the rest of the group's needs. Student contributes little or nothing to the research and development of the presentation.

W: The student's work is unacceptable, with little or no participation in any aspect of the activity.

X: The student's work is poor, with no contributions to the group effort.

21st Century Learning

Technology Extension: Online Opinion Polls

Using online survey tools allows students to easily collect and aggregate data in multiple formats for analysis. In addition, many online tools provide the opportunity to receive feedback not just from students in class, but from surrounding communities that may include parents, relatives, and other teachers. The creation of a clear and articulate survey also requires that students thoughtfully present written statements and questions to their audience in a clear and concise manner.

Online surveys are an easy and quick way to gather feedback. These tools do not require any prior programming or online development skills and may be accessed via a link on a Web site, wiki, blog, social network, or in an e-mail. In this EdTechTeacher Technology Extension, we'll provide the resources for your students to learn how to create online surveys that they can use as part of their project to assess President Reagan's job performance.

Creating Online Surveys

There are several free programs that allow students to design, build, and distribute online surveys. To learn more about creating online surveys, visit the Student Response Systems page at EdTechTeacher's Teaching History with Technology site: http://thwt.org/multimedia/polls-surveys/. On this page you'll find an overview of online surveys, examples of online surveys, links to online survey creation tools, and a series of video tutorials for designing online surveys.

Creating online surveys is completely free, so have fun and practice with your students prior to designing the surveys for this Learning Technology Extension.

Creating Online Surveys of President Reagan

Activate student background knowledge by tasking small groups to review the material presented in Lesson 1 and compile a list of issues that were most important to Americans in the 1980s. As a class, discuss the issues and create a list on the board.

Have small groups choose five issues from the class list or their own brainstorming session, and compose five statements that assess President Reagan's job performance on these issues. Explain to students that they will be conducting their surveys online and that the statements must be clear and concise.

Each group should identify at least ten survey takers who were of voting age in the 1980s. This provides a manageable amount of information and accounts for some incomplete surveys. You should be prepared with additional names in case students find this difficult.

Open your sample survey and review the basic functionality with your students. Each student group should create one account and then develop their online surveys. Have each group provide peer feedback to another group on the quality of the statements as well as the general layout of the surveys. Groups should incorporate this feedback and finalize their surveys.

Completed surveys can now be embedded in emails, a class wiki, blog or web site. These can then be distributed to potential survey respondents.

Allow time for the results to be gathered and then have students review their data. A great advantage to online surveys is that the data will be accessible to students from anywhere. This way they can review responses at various locations and come to class better prepared to discuss with their groups.

Ask students to calculate the average response to each of their statements and then write a brief paragraph for each in which they attempt to interpret their findings. Online survey tools will provide many graphical representations of the data that students should use when reporting their findings to the entire class. You can also have students share or aggregate their findings, and have a final class discussion where students discuss and process what their results mean for Reagan's legacy.

Assessment and Rubrics

You can create evaluation categories for the quality of their statements and questions, level of peer feedback, analysis of the results, summary paragraphs and their class presentations. For more information about creating rubrics, visit http://thwt.org/rubrics.html.

Additional Online Resources

For more Web sites, lesson plans, and activities related to the resurgence of conservatism in the United States and the fall of communism in the Soviet Union, visit the Cold War Era section of Best of History Websites: http://besthistorysites.net/american-history/cold-war-era/.

Hands-On History Chapter Project

A Time of Change, 1980–2000

Art Show

Step 1: Researching the History of the Period

Directions Explain to students that they are going to create an art show of at least 10 images that they will hang in the classroom, a school hall, or foyer, complete with a title, brief introduction and accompanying explanatory tags that will identify the images. In this step, two teams of students will: a) describe the events occurring in the United States between 1980 and 2000; and b) depict themes of the period. Each team will discuss how to depict the subject using images. Students may choose to use graphic organizers, maps, charts, paintings, or drawings. Students may create their own images or find historical images online or in the library.

Putting It Together After the two teams have determined four or five image selections, they should each either obtain the images (photocopies) or sketch them in a rough draft.

Step 2: Selecting the Images for the Art Exhibit

Ask: How do the selected images reflect the period? What is most important about them?

Directions Student teams will continue to create their images. In this step, students will determine which members of their team will create the informational tags that will accompany the images in the art show. The informational tags should be typed sheets that include the following information:

- Image title
- Brief summary of how the image relates to the historical period
- Media (oil, watercolor, drawing, and so on)
- Date of completion
- Any other pertinent information

Putting It Together In one or two sittings, students should review the submissions and decide which will be hung in the exhibit. School policy and space may determine if this ends up being an actual exhibit or a virtual exhibit.

Hands-On History Chapter Project *Cont.*

A Time of Change, 1980–2000

Step 3: Hanging the Show

Ask: How should the images best be presented to illustrate this time of change in American history?

Directions The final job is to hang the show, but this requires decisions about the best order in which to present the images for the audience. Students may choose to hang the images by chronological order, by date of the artwork, by the artists, or by a perceived theme in the images. Another task is to review the informational tags that will accompany the images. Will the tags give the audience enough information to see the topic clearly?

Putting It Together If there is space for the show to be hung; getting the materials to hang it is the last step. Students from other classes might view it and review it.

Step 4: Wrap-Up After students have hung the presentation, they will acquire feedback and learn from the feedback.

Directions After the audience has had a chance to review the art show, ask them for their feedback. (You may want to put comment cards out for audience members.) As a class, review the comments, as well as discuss your own reactions to the show.

Ask the following questions to start the discussion:

- What was good about the show?

- Did the images illustrate the topics clearly? Why or why not?

- How could the show have been improved?

- What would you do differently if you did this project again?

Putting It Together As a final close to the project, have students write a brief summary of their reactions to the project, explaining how it illustrated the time period.

Assessing Tell students that their presentation will be assessed based on these factors:

S: Student participates fully and actively in each group of which he or she is a member. Student contributes to all discussions and decision-making in both the smaller group and in the group as a whole. In all activities and research, student exhibits an excellent understanding of how to research and develop the multimedia presentation, of the steps needed in acquiring information and in how to build and present the presentation. Students demonstrate an understanding of how to best display the information and the content of the information does not show grammar flaws or sloppy, incomplete work.

T: Student participates in both the smaller group and the larger class. The student participates in the research and development of the presentation. Students show some understanding of the creation and the content in the presentation.

U: Student participates very little in the group and does little research. The student also has limited input into the research and development of the multimedia presentation that is created.

Hands-On History Chapter Project *Cont.*

A Time of Change, 1980–2000

V: Student rarely participates in any groups, does incomplete and unsatisfactory research and development work, and offers little in the way of input to the rest of the group's needs. Student contributes little or nothing to the research and development of the presentation.

W: The student's work is unacceptable, with little or no participation in any aspect of the activity.

X: The student's work is poor, with no contributions to the group effort.

Technology Extension: Online Art Show with Wikis

When students create an art show online, they are able to share their work with the wider school community, as well as develop their multimedia creation skills. Giving students the opportunity to publish their work online provides them with an engaging, authentic learning experience, and they often surprise their teachers with the high quality of work that they produce in online venues.

Wikis are terrific platforms for creating collaborative online art exhibits. A wiki is a Web site where students can collaboratively create Web pages through an interface similar to a word processing program, and that does not require any special programming skills. In this EdTechTeacher Technology Extension, we will provide the resources for you to learn how to use wikis so that your students can publish their art show online.

Creating Wikis

There are several wiki hosting services that allow K-12 teachers to set up wikis and subscribe their students as editors entirely for free. To learn more about creating and setting up wikis, visit the Collaborating with Wikis page at EdTechTeacher's Teaching History with Technology site: http://thwt.org/discussion-collaboration/wikis/. On this page you will find an overview of how to use wikis, examples of wikis created by other classroom history teachers, links to wiki hosting platforms, and a series of video tutorials for creating and managing wikis.

Since creating wikis can be done for free, create a test wiki and play around with the features and settings before you create your "real" classroom art show project wiki.

Creating an Art Show with Wikis

Once you have created a wiki for students to publish their art show, you will need to create a Planning Page and an Exhibit Page for each group in your class. The Planning Page will be where groups collect their research, take notes, and plan their exhibit. The Exhibit Page will display the final product.

The first two pages are the team Planning Pages:

- Have each group complete Step 1 on their team planning page: including notes on the events occurring in the United States between 1980 and 2000, themes of that period, descriptions of images, collected resources, and group and individual task lists.

  - *One advantage of wikis is that they can be accessed from anywhere, so students do not have to worry about losing their materials if they work on the project from school, from home, and from the library!*

- Students should now complete Step 2 by gathering their images and multimedia that reflects their content from Step 1.

- Even if students still create real-world exhibits, like dioramas, statues, or display boards, these can be photographed with a digital camera and documented online.

- Each image should include informational tags with the following:

  - Image title

  - Brief summary of how the image relates to the historical period

  - Media (oil, watercolor, drawing, and so on)

- Date of completion

- Any other pertinent information

- Have students post their bibliography on this page.

- Finally, students can create a mock-up of their group vision for the art show.

Students groups will now come together to review the Planning Page and decide which images will be included in the class art show. This is a great opportunity for students to collaborate and negotiate with each other on what to include and how to present their images. It is clear students understand they are one team and that the final product will reflect the effort of the whole class.

The third page is the final Exhibit Page:

- Here each group can publish its final exhibit online, including titles, images, brief introductions, and explanatory tags.

Most wiki platforms have a "Comment" or "Discussion" page associated with each content page. Encourage your students to direct their visitors to leave a comment about their art show experience.

- *This is a great way to have family members, schoolmates, and other community members participate in the art show.*

As a class, review the comments, as well as discuss your own reactions to the art show. Ask the following questions to start the discussion:

- What was good about the show?

- Did the images illustrate the topics clearly? Why or why not?

- How could the show have been improved?

- What would you do differently if you did this project again?

As a final close to the project, have students write and post a brief summary of their reactions to the project, explaining how it illustrated the time period.

Assessment and Rubrics

You can create evaluation categories for students' use of the multimedia features of wikis, their image selections, descriptions, collaboration, and analysis. One advantage of grading and assessing work completed on wikis is that wikis maintain a historical record of every edit made to every page (look on the "History" tab). These edit records allow you to gauge accurately how much each individual team member contributed to the overall project. For guidance on creating rubrics, see the Teaching History with Technology rubric page at http://thwt.org/rubrics.html.

Additional Online Resources

Citation Tools: To help students with their citation, you might encourage them to use one of several online citation generators. For more on these free, online tools, visit the Citation page at Teaching History with Technology: http://thwt.org/citation.html.

Hands-On History Chapter Project

America's Challenges for a New Century, 2001–2008

Exploring the "Blogosphere"

ESSENTIAL QUESTIONS
- *How is American culture shaped by a set of common values and practices?*
- *How have disputes over ideas, values, and politics resulted in change?*

Step 1: Making a Blog Chart Groups of students will search the Internet to identify a variety of blogs. They will chart the information.

Directions Tell groups of students to use a search engine to find blogs on different topics. Groups will then chart the information they have collected in three columns. The first column will give the name and Web address of the blog. The second column will describe the topic of the blog. Topics may cover a range of subjects—from politics to pop culture. The third column will cite what kind of blog it is (private, political, or commercial) and its creator's name.

Putting It Together Have students share what they learned about how people use the Internet to communicate. Encourage the class to speculate about the goals of each of the blogs on their charts.

Step 2: Blog Quotes Students will make posters using quotes from blogs selected from the chart they compiled in Step 1.

Directions Have student groups select a quote from three of the blogs found on their charts. Ask students to make a poster for each quote. Each poster should include the quote in large enough type to be read easily. The posters should also include photographs from newspapers, magazines, and the Internet that illustrate the meaning of the quote.

Putting It Together Have students present their posters to the class. Ask the class to match the posters to blogs on the chart compiled in Step 1. Have them discuss in what ways, if any, the blogs from which they have quoted strengthen or threaten democracy.

Step 3: Blogging Students will work in groups to create their own blog.

Directions Write the Essential Questions on the board. Remind students that they have the responsibility to practice free speech in a constructive manner. Any criticism they make should be useful and not abusive. Have student groups use the charts and posters they created in Steps 1 and 2 to brainstorm ideas for a blog topic. Remind students that the content of their blog must meet school standards. When students have selected a topic and a name for their blogs, have them collaborate on writing the first entries for their blogs.

Hands-On History Chapter Project *Cont.*

America's Challenges for a New Century, 2001–2008

Putting It Together Have students read their blog entries to the class. Encourage the class to discuss how they chose their blog topics and how school standards influenced what they wrote.

Step 4: Responding to Blogs Student groups respond to blog entries created in Step 3.

Directions Have student groups trade the blogs they created in Step 3. As a group, have students write a response to the blog entry. Remind students that readers contribute to blogs in many ways. They may rebut opinions stated in blogs. Sometimes they add helpful information such as links. They may point out errors in information and make corrections. Sometimes they may simply express admiration for the blog. Have students weigh their right to free speech with their responsibility for civility as they respond to each other's blogs.

Putting It Together Have groups share their blog responses with the class. Encourage the class to discuss what they learned about the Essential Questions of this chapter as they explored the "blogosphere."

Step 5: Wrap-Up Students will write an informational essay on blogs.

Directions Direct students to write an essay in which they use what they have learned in Steps 1 through 4 of this project. Student essays should answer the following questions:

- What are blogs?

- What purpose do blogs serve in today's society?

- Are blogs beneficial to U.S. society? Why or why not?

- What other purposes might blogs be used for to benefit society?

Putting It Together Students should write and turn in their essays individually; however, you may want to share interesting responses with the entire class.

Assessing Tell students that their presentation will be assessed based on these factors:

S: Student participates fully and actively in each group of which he or she is a member. Student contributes to all discussions and decision-making in both the smaller group and in the group as a whole. In all activities and research, student exhibits an excellent understanding of how to research and develop the multimedia presentation, of the steps needed in acquiring information and in how to build and present the presentation. Students demonstrate an understanding of how to best display the information and the content of the information does not show grammar flaws or sloppy, incomplete work.

T: Student participates in both the smaller group and the larger class. The student participates in the research and development of the presentation. Students show some understanding of the creation and the content in the presentation.

U: Student participates very little in the group and does little research. The student also has limited input into the research and development of the multimedia presentation that is created.

Hands-On History Chapter Project *Cont.*

America's Challenges for a New Century, 2001–2008

V: Student rarely participates in any groups, does incomplete and unsatisfactory research and development work, and offers little in the way of input to the rest of the group's needs. Student contributes little or nothing to the research and development of the presentation.

W: The student's work is unacceptable, with little or no participation in any aspect of the activity.

X: The student's work is poor, with no contributions to the group effort.

Technology Extension: Blogs

A blog is a great way for students to practice literacy skills in an authentic environment. Having your students turn their written work into published blogs will provide them with a sense of accomplishment, while opening up student work to the entire class, school, or wider community for peer editing and instruction. When students know that their writing will be viewed by others, they are more motivated to do their best. The ability to organize content easily and offer comments makes this tool a wonderfully collaborative and generative addition to your class.

The term 'blog' came from a blending of the words 'Web' and 'log' because it is simply an online format for keeping records. Personal diary-type entries, commentaries, news events, links, photographs, and videos are just some of the things that bloggers share. Blogs can easily be adapted for use in the classroom through a variety of free online services. In this EdTechTeacher Technology Extension, we will provide resources and tips to help your students analyze the "blogosphere."

Creating Blogs

There are many free, simple blog creation and hosting Web sites that you can use to create your students' blogs. For more information about educational blogging, visit Teaching History with Technology's (THWT) blogging page at http://thwt.org/historyblogs.html. This page contains additional reasons and methods for using blogs in the history classroom, as well as detailed information and tutorials about some of the most popular blogging Web sites. You will also find information related to privacy and student work on the Internet.

Supporting your Blog Project

To best support your Hands-On Chapter Project, here are some additional tips and recommendations:

To aid in activating your students' background knowledge, have your students discuss the kinds of blogs they read and the qualities that make for a good blog entry or a good comment. As a class, view examples and exemplars of student blogs at the THWT blogging page.

In small groups, have your students use a blog search engine, like http://www.blogsearchengine.org/, to identify a variety of blogs for analysis. Task them to create the three-column chart described in the Hands-On Chapter Project plan.

- As a class have students speculate about the goals of the blogs and whether or not they believe these goals have been accomplished.

- Also ask them: What makes the authors' messages unique to this format?

After completing Step 2, the posters, and discussing the impact of blogs on democracy, task groups to create their own blog. Have student groups use the charts and posters they created to brainstorm ideas for a blog topic. Remind students that the content of their blog must meet school standards.

Once you have chosen the blog site that you want to use, you will want to create a sample blog or template to show students as an example and to familiarize yourself with the process. Practice formatting, editing, and commenting on a blog entry in order to anticipate students' questions. Have students select a topic and a name for their blogs.

As groups create their blogs, each group should create a "blogroll" on their blog's sidebar; a blogroll is a list of links to all of blogs of the other groups in the class. This allows students to easily click through to visit each other's blogs. It also makes it easier for you, as teacher, to quickly visit all of your groups' blogs as they are developing.

Have each group collaborate to write the first entry for their blogs. After groups finish their posts, discuss them as a class and task students to leave comments on two other blogs. You can have an entire, asynchronous "class discussion" that takes place online. To help hold students accountable for closely reading each other's blogs, review their comments in class and have them explain why they responded in a particular way. Also, have students weigh their right to free speech with their responsibility for civility as they respond to each other's blogs.

To continue the transparency in the Wrap Up phase, you can ask students to attach their final essays to their groups' blogs. At this time you may choose to make your class blogs viewable to a wider audience and request feedback from family, friends or the educational community.

Assessment and Rubrics

To create a rubric to assess students' blogs, visit the Rubric page at EdTechTeacher's Teaching History with Technology site: http://thwt.org/rubrics.html

Hands-On History Chapter Project

Obama and Beyond, 2008–Present

Sharing News through Social Media

ESSENTIAL QUESTIONS
- *How does social media affect how news is shared?*
- *How have disputes over ideas, values, and politics resulted in change?*

Step 1: Exploring the Impact of Social Media

Directions Explain to students that they will create a presentation that compares how a local or national newspaper provides news through social media updates versus how it provides news through a "traditional" article. Students will create a timeline that shows a side-by-side comparison of each update and tracks whether the news communicated in the update ultimately appears in an article. They should take note of how many original updates the account provides as well as updates that the account reposts from other people.

Begin by asking students to define the term "citizen journalism" (the collection, dissemination, and analysis of news and information by the general public, especially by means of the Internet). Point out to students that many media outlets encourage viewers to be "citizen journalists" and share photos and personal observations when they happen to be at the scene of a newsworthy event.

Putting it Together Students should first select a local or national newspaper. They should then go online to find the paper's official Web site and social media account. Students should follow the social media account for one full day, noting a.) how often the account is updated, b.) how many original updates the site provides along compared with those posts provided by citizen journalists—either through submissions or reposts from other accounts. Students will then create a timeline that shows how the string of updates compares to the news article that appears on the official site.

Step 2: Editing and Presenting

Ask: What is the essential core of the presentation to be preserved, and what introduction and conclusion needs to be added to it?

Directions Students will need to work together to determine which updates are most important to include in the timeline. They will also need to collectively write an introduction and conclusion for the final product. The tasks can be divided among the students according to their interests and skills. Then students should do a final edit of the presentation by asking themselves:

- Did I give a good introduction?

- Are the questions and answers clear to my audience?

Hands-On History Chapter Project *Cont.*

Obama and Beyond, 2008–Present

- What conclusions should be drawn from the information given?

- Did I summarize the timeline or provide a closing statement?

Putting it Together Presenters should be prepared for follow-up questions from their audience. They should be sure that they have researched the topics covered in the presentation.

Step 3: Wrap-Up Students will review the presentations and provide an evaluation of their work.

Directions Students follow up their presentations with a self-evaluation of both the project and their work in it. Students should write a brief essay that answers the questions below.

- What was the most difficult part of this project? Why?

- What was the best part of this project? Why?

- What could be done to improve the presentation?

- What did I learn about war by completing this project?

Putting it Together Students should provide clear essays and succinct answers to each question above.

Assessing Tell students that their presentation will be assessed based on these factors:

S: Student participates fully and actively in each group of which he or she is a member. Student contributes to all discussions and decision-making in both the smaller group and in the group as a whole. In all activities and research, student exhibits an excellent understanding of how to research and develop the multimedia presentation, of the steps needed in acquiring information and in how to build and present the presentation. Students demonstrate an understanding of how to best display the information and the content of the information does not show grammar flaws or sloppy, incomplete work.

T: Student participates in both the smaller group and the larger class. The student participates in the research and development of the presentation. Students show some understanding of the creation and the content in the presentation.

U: Student participates very little in the group and does little research. The student also has limited input into the research and development of the multimedia presentation that is created.

V: Student rarely participates in any groups, does incomplete and unsatisfactory research and development work, and offers little in the way of input to the rest of the group's needs. Student contributes little or nothing to the research and development of the presentation.

W: The student's work is unacceptable, with little or no participation in any aspect of the activity.

X: The student's work is poor, with no contributions to the group effort.

Technology Extension: Digital Time Line

Understanding how to read and create a time line is a useful social studies skill that enhances a student's ability to see the chronology of events and make educated guesses about how events connect to one another and influence one another.

Today, there are many ways to create digital time lines that can enhance understanding of events with photos or more complex interactivity. These time lines may include images, video, audio, hyperlinks, and other ways to deepen the content organized in a time line fashion. Most digital time lines can be embedded in existing Web pages or wikis and can be shared via social networking services. Students can collaborate online and help create content material for their classmates as well. There are various online platforms that allow users to create, publish, and share digital time lines. In this EdTechTeacher Technology Extension, we'll provide the resources that allow you to learn how to use these platforms to help your students create a digital time line of events in contemporary United States history.

Creating Digital Time Lines

As with most platforms, online digital time lines differ in the extent of what users can do and how they can develop their finished product. In most platforms, users log in using a valid e-mail address and are presented with a blank page for their work. There may be a simple set of step-by-step instructions that aid you in getting started with your basic time line content entry. Images are usually uploaded, so students should collect their image files in a common folder for organization and easy upload. Most platforms have a few choices of layouts and backgrounds, and may offer themes.

Before entering information, students should gather the number of entries they are providing and determine basic details such as the start date and end date of the time line, as well as an appropriate interval of time between entries. Students should be cautioned about getting too caught up in the design details and losing focus on the historical content. Assessment rubrics should reflect the importance of content over style.

To learn more about these platforms and creating time lines, visit the time lines page at EdTechTeacher's Teaching History with Technology site: http://thwt.org/multimedia/timelines/.

On this page you'll find links to time line platforms, an overview of why time lines are useful, and examples of online time lines created by other classroom history teachers.

Creating a Digital Time Line for Contemporary Events

This project can be used as an extension for the Hands-On Chapter Project "Sharing News through Citizen Journalism and Social Media" time line or as a substitution. Students should follow the same procedure described for developing the project. Almost all time line platforms require a login with an active e-mail account, and some allow teachers to create a class account for collaboration. Users can invite others to share on most platforms. Consult the various platforms in order to decide the approach to students logging in to the chosen platform.

Students should plan on creating a digital time line that highlights the same events they identified in making the Hands-On Chapter Project time line. The time line should contain a suitable number of entries, a summary statement of the entry, a chronological date for each entry, and additional digital enhancement that takes advantage of the functionality given in an online time line: additional photos, more room for text, hyperlinks between events, additional video or music, or new display options. Students should also pay attention to the "look" of the time line, selecting a theme, color scheme, and additional flourishes that apply to the topic.

Students must be sure to record the source of all images or other media used in the creation of their time line, which can be listed in a separate document or possibly in a field for each item entry. This may depend on the different options provided by the online platform that is chosen. The final time lines can be collected and displayed through embedding or hyperlinks on a class Web site or wiki. In addition, the time lines can be presented in class and used as the basis for a discussion about contemporary issues in the final chapter.

Assessment and Rubrics

The project should be assessed based on historical content, use of visuals, and presentation and mechanics, and collaboration if required. For advice on creating a rubric to assess digital time lines, visit the Rubric page at EdTechTeacher's Teaching History with Technology site: http://thwt.org/rubrics.html.

Additional Online Resources

For more online activities related to contemporary events, visit McGraw-Hill Education's btw: Stuff You Should Know Web site: http://blog.mheonline.com/btw. Or use commercial journalism Web sites for additional details about current news events.